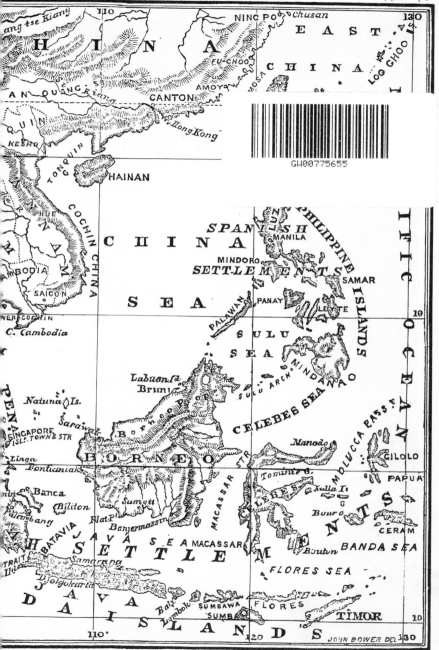

CHINA

NINC PO chusan

EAST

FU-CHOO

CHINA

AMOY

AN QUANG Kiang   CANTON

FORMOSA

LOO CHOO

QUIN

Hong Kong

KESHO

TONQUIN

HUE

COCHIN CHINA

HAINAN

CAMBODIA

SAIGON

CHINA

SPANISH

MINDORO

SETTLEMENTS

MANILA

PHILIPPINE ISLANDS

SAMAR

PANAY

LEYTE

NERECOCHIN

C. Cambodia

SEA

PALAWAN

SULU

SEA

SULU ARCH.

MINDANAO

CELEBES SEA

Labuan Id
Bruni

MOLUCCA PASS

GILOLO

Natuna Is.

Sarawak

PEN

SINGAPORE
ISL. TOWN & STR

BORNEO

Manado

PAPUA

Tomine G.

Linga

Pontianak

Xulla Is

Banca

Biliton

Sumou

Flat Pt

Banjermassin

MACASSAR STR.

CELEBES

Buuro

CERAM

BATAVIA

JAVA

SETTLE

S E A MACASSAR

MENTS

BANDA SEA

Samarang

Djokjokarta

FLORES SEA

JAVA

ISLANDS

Bali

Lomboko

SUMBAWA

FLORES

SUMBA

TIMOR

JOHN BOWER DEL

IMAGES OF ASIA
Series Adviser: SYLVIA FRASER-LU

Old Penang

Titles in the series

The genus *Areca catechu*, commonly known as the betel-nut palm, from
A Garden of Eden: Plant Life in South-East Asia, by W. Veevers-Carter,
Singapore, Oxford University Press, 1986.

Old Penang

SARNIA HAYES HOYT

SINGAPORE
OXFORD UNIVERSITY PRESS
OXFORD NEW YORK
1991

Oxford University Press

Oxford New York Toronto
Delhi Bombay Calcutta Madras Karachi
Petaling Jaya Singapore Hong Kong Tokyo
Nairobi Dar es Salaam Cape Town
Melbourne Auckland
amd associated companies in
Berlin Ibadan

Oxford is a trade mark of Oxford University Press

© Oxford University Press Pte. Ltd. 1991

Published in the United States by
Oxford University Press Inc., New York

ISBN 0 19 588551 1

British Library Cataloguing-in-Publication Data

A catalogue record for this book is
available from the British Library

Library of Congress Cataloging-in-Publication Data

Hoyt, Sarnia Hayes, 1938–
Old Penang/Sarnia Hayes Hoyt.
p.   cm.—(Images of Asia)
Includes bibliographical references and index.
ISBN 0–19–588551–1:
1. Pinang—History. I. Title.   II. Series.
DS598.P5H69 1991
959.5'1—dc20
91–21629
CIP

Printed in Singapore by Kim Hup Lee Printing Co. Pte. Ltd.
Published by Oxford University Press Pte. Ltd.,
Unit 221, Ubi Avenue 4, Singapore 1440

To the memory of my mother
Margaret Kidder Hayes
who first wrote to me

Preface

As a history student in the America of the late 1950s, my understanding of South-East Asia was limited to the romance of the white planter as told by Somerset Maugham. When I arrived in Singapore early in 1989 I had a chance to correct this Eurocentric myopia and begin to acquire an Asian perspective.

A circuitous route to Penang involved an assignment in Holland where we dined often at a neighbourhood Amsterdam bistro owned by Kim and Robert Hollauf. Robert, an Austrian, cooked splendid meals while his wife Kim took orders, uncorked the wine, and chatted with guests. Kim came from Penang.

Two years later in Singapore, we met more people from Penang—bankers, architects, lawyers, teachers. What was the origin of this remarkable diaspora, I wondered. Meanwhile, I had discovered Straits Chinese porcelain and had met an American collector in a Hong Kong antique shop. When she suggested Penang for the best buys, I had to go.

We checked into the E & O Hotel and spent a weekend as tourists exploring George Town's shophouse-lined streets which, happily, are not sanitized for tourists. They are, rather, pleasantly chaotic and authentic. We photographed temples and mosques, squeezed into a trishaw for a terrifying tour through Penang traffic, ate bowls of noodles, and watched the sunset glow over Kedah's peaks from a cool lookout on Penang Hill.

What started as a touristic visit to Malaysia in pursuit of Straits Chinese porcelain has, with the help and encouragement of the Oxford University Press, become a little book. It is the result of a year of regular trips to Penang, many delightful evenings with new friends there who introduced me to the distinct pleasures of Penang food, and months in the libraries and museums of Penang and Singapore. It is the work of a native New Yorker for whom urban racial tensions seem all too normal and who found in Penang, where diversity and harmony are not mutually exclusive, a sense of hope.

While researching and writing I have consulted many people who have been generous with their time in interviews and conversations. They have directed me to sources of information I might have missed, loaned books, sent articles, offered advice and criticism, and read portions of the manuscript. I would like to mention, in particular, Michael J. Sweet, Arthur Khoo, Chew Mee Kirtland, Andrew Tan, Tai Lung Ee, Chuah Qeng Eng, Joceline Tan, Dr Leong Yee Fong, Kenneth Cheo, Dr Ghulam Sarwar Yousof, Andrew Aeria, Michael and June Quah, Martin Khor, Kathleen Hunink, Mary Yeoh, Dr Jon Lim, Lesley Layton, Maya Jayapal, Datuk Khor Cheang Kee, Dr Chandra Muzaffar, Tan Thean Siew, and Brian Cooper.

To Datuk Lim Chong Keat, whose *Penang Views* first opened my eyes to the beauties of old Penang, and the librarians at the Southeast Asia Room at the National Library of Singapore, I owe a special word of thanks.

I wish also to express my appreciation to the following for granting permission to use many of the illustrations that accompany the text: Michael J. Sweet at Antiques of the Orient in Singapore, Major David Ng, Raymond Brammah, Penang Museum and Art Gallery, National Museum of Singapore, Longman Malaysia, Raffles Hotel Heritage Collection, Brigadier G. H. Cree, Datuk Khoo Keat Siew, and W. Veevers-Carter.

My task would have been more difficult without the help of Marianita G. Fumar.

Finally, this project would not have been possible without my husband Edward who persuaded me to come to South-East Asia in the first place, and then backed me every step of the way.

Singapore   SARNIA HAYES HOYT
March 1991

Contents

I

Introduction

SEEN from the air, Penang floats like a small turtle—a total of 280 square kilometres—off the edge of Peninsular Malaysia, at the northern end of the Straits of Malacca (Plate 1). The city of George Town, located on the most eastern cape of the island, reaches out towards Butterworth and the Penang ferry terminal, which is about 3.2 kilometres away on the mainland.

During the sixteenth century, Portuguese sailors and traders called the island Pulo Pinaom for the 'pinang' or areca nut palm tree probably cultivated there then. This tree, commonly known as the betel-nut palm, or *pokok pinang* in Malay, still grows there and has given its Malay name *pinang*, or 'penang' in English, to the island (Frontispiece).

Fruits of the betel-nut palm play an important symbolic role in Malay culture and were adopted by the Straits Chinese in traditional marriage ceremonies. Nuts growing in large bunches at the top of the straight, slender trunk are shaved into small pieces and, together with fresh palm leaves, lime, and cloves, form an aromatic chewing mixture which colours the lips and saliva red. The custom of chewing this quid, derived from India, became popular in South-East Asia for its pleasantly narcotic effects.

The British named the island Prince of Wales Island for the future George IV, but this name was dropped after Malayan independence in 1957. They also named the principal settlement George Town for his reigning father, George III, and although this name still appears in guidebooks and maps, it is not consistently used now. Some

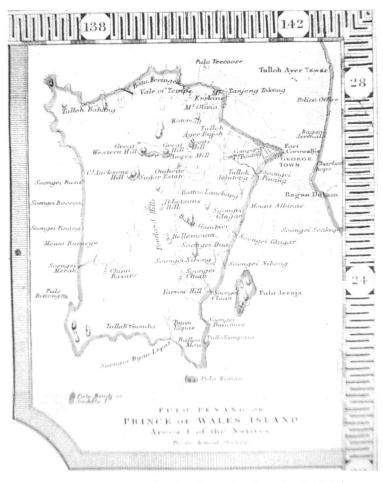

1. 'Pulo Penang or Prince of Wales Island', by Alexander Keith Johnston, geographer to Queen Victoria, from the National Atlas, Edinburgh, 1849. (Antiques of the Orient)

Penangites use the Malay word for cape, *tanjung*, to refer to the only city on the island. They also say the name for the whole island—Penang—to refer to the urban part of it.

Today, regular ferry services between Penang and Butterworth, a 13.5-kilometre bridge, and an international airport at Bayan Lepas connect the island with Peninsular Malaysia and other parts of the world. But during most of the 150-year period covered by this little book, immigrants and travellers to Penang approached the island by boat from the mainland or after a long sea voyage across the Bay of Bengal or through the Straits. Navigators preferred the north channel because it was deeper than the southern one. Ships entered the harbour, a 4.5-kilometre stretch between the mainland and the island, after passing the lighthouse at Muka Head and the northern beaches.

Sir Frank Swettenham, Resident-General of the Federated Malay States, described the arrival at Penang in 1907: '... and then, in a moment, there is the town, and the ship seems to be running into its main street. The white buildings and red roofs, which house a hundred thousand people, crammed closely together on the flat tongue of land that stretches, from the foot of Pinang Hill, right out into the Strait which divides it from the mainland, just as though the island were ever trying to get its foot back on the opposite shore. And when the red roofs cease to catch the eye as a mass, they twinkle at you, here and there, from the foliage of garden and orchard, till all is merged in green and purple against the background of that great hill.'

From the water—blue, grey, or pale gold depending on the light—about a third of the island appears to be a flat plain, but a range of granite hills over 610 metres high covers about a quarter of its surface and gives it the outline, some travellers said, of a hog's back or of a great whale basking in the sea. The coastline of the island's southern

3

end, like that of the west Malay coast, consists of mangrove swamps and mud flats alternating with palm-fringed bays.

For the passenger, disembarkation meant new sensory experience. The wharf was 'like a beehive, crowded with Chinese coolies and Tamils with their bullock carts'. Along the quay, ingots of tin were stacked awaiting shipment, together with rubber and copra. The sweet nutty smell of drying coconut mingled with the stink of the monsoon drains and the scent of cloves and pepper—spicy odours of the Far East. The streets echoed with the clip clop of wooden clogs worn by Chinese women and hawkers selling local delicacies—'*Nasi lemak*!'

At 625 kilometres north of the Equator, temperatures in the lowlands of Penang are always hot, ranging between 26 °C and 32 °C. Life here is slow but nature is fast; the sun rises and sets quickly, and violent storms can come and go within an hour. Rainfall varies with two annual monsoon seasons which mean drier months from December to March and in June and July. Average annual rainfall in 1900 was about 317 centimetres.

At these latitudes, 'dry' is a relative term. As James Low, a nineteenth-century visitor said, 'The air in Penang is saturated with moisture, and acts as a lens. The radiant caloric is not driven off by the wind.' In 1852, Charles Kinloch counted only six houses in George Town that enjoyed the sea breeze.

The evidence of early maps shows that Portuguese sailors were not the only visitors to Penang. Indian, Arabian, Chinese, Dutch, Danish, and French ships, as well as those from the Malay Archipelago probably put into its protected harbour during the monsoons.

The first recorded British visit to the island took place in 1592 when James Lancaster, captain of the *Edward Bonaventure*, dropped anchor at Penang. He and his sailors, many sick with scurvy, rested here for several weeks, taking on water and enjoying fresh oysters.

With the health of his own men on his mind, Lancaster's journals said nothing about people living on the island. Yet during this period—for 500 years, in fact—the island was part of Kedah, a Muslim state sharing a long border with Siam, and the discovery of eighteenth-century burial grounds on Penang has confirmed the existence of a native community. Pirates also lived on the island until the Sultan of Kedah drove them out, first in 1750, and again in 1786, the year the British settlers arrived. Another engraving by Captain Elisha Trapaud, who witnessed the British flag-raising ceremony in August 1786 (Plate 2), depicted Malay-style homes of fifty-eight people said to be living on the island in 1786.

The Sultan of Kedah helped the British clear land by sending some able-bodied men, who were followed quickly by people from all parts of the Malay Archipelago, and later from south China and India. They became the backbone of Penang. They built roads and houses, caught and sold fish, pulled rickshaws (Plate 3), managed draught animals, grew fruits and vegetables, worked plantations and tin smelters, loaded and unloaded ships, and washed clothes. Yet the voice of the peoples of the region is rarely heard.

When the British took over the island they began in their letters to East India Company officials in Calcutta and London what would become a voluminous record of the settlement, which they considered part of British India. But this record of Penang, supplemented by later European vis-itors, is not balanced by the candid Asian perspective of another Munshi Abdullah, who was Malacca's Malay author of an early nineteenth-century chronicle.

Modern readers will find most of these civil servants and travellers ethnocentric, narrow-minded, and judgemental.

2. 'View of the North Point of the Prince of Wales's Island & the Ceremony of Christening it', engraving by Captain Elisha Trapaud, 1786.

3. Jinrickishas from China came into general use in Penang after 1895.
(Major David Ng)

Chinese architecture, according to a 1924 travel guide, was 'peculiar'. The adjective 'European' is used as a synonym for 'superior'. Maintaining their position by prestige, not military force, many Europeans believed they enjoyed the good life in the East—large salaries with fine houses and servants—because they really were a superior race.

Although some visitors to Penang commented on the proximity of native and European homes, Europeans and Asians during the colonial period lived in two different worlds. According to Governor Bannerman (quoted in Wong Lin Ken), the natives in 1818 were 'too remote from civilization and far too unfit from education and habits to justify the smallest comparison being made between them and Europeans'. Races other than the Malays and the

Chinese do not have what would be considered a social life, explained another European. They are simply 'hewers of wood and drawers of water'. Even during the late 1920s, George Bilainkin, a newspaper editor working in Penang, was shocked to discover that when he entertained a Chinese guest on the E & O Hotel's seafront terrace, he was snubbed by other Europeans.

Readers should be aware that pictorial evidence and the written record perpetuate certain racial stereotypes. The Indians are always 'docile' and 'cringing', the Chinese are 'the bone and sinew of the colony—industrious, but crafty', and the Malays are 'lazy', 'half-naked', and 'copper coloured'. They must remember that there were also Indian teachers and lawyers, Chinese businessmen–philanthropists, and gifted Malay actors, dancers, craftsmen, and writers. Readers must know, too, that not all Europeans enjoyed a comfortable lifestyle. Many came East on missionary or educational impulses and lived close to the people they served.

And as they read Europeans' accounts of arrivals at Penang harbour, readers should imagine what might have been written by an indentured Indian labourer or convict, or a new arrival from China (a *sinkeh*) who would be inspected on shipboard by a coolie trader looking for the healthiest men to sell, like meat on the hoof (Plate 4).

Occasionally, when listening hard, one hears another point of view. Asians seem superior in 'deportment', wrote Bilainkin, because they don't chatter in public the way Europeans do. Snapping fingers to get the attention of the 'head boy' is not appropriate in hotel restaurants, said a visitor in the 1930s, who didn't like the term 'boy' for a responsible *maître d'hôtel*. Another commented sadly on whole families of homeless Tamils—'seven children and parents huddled together in a line'—living only 200 metres from his hotel.

1714 the British navy was larger and more effectively
administered than Holland's, while British cartography and
shipbuilding became the best in the world. The Dutch
position, gradually undermined by internal weaknesses, no
longer posed a serious threat.

At the same time, new global conflicts were forcing the
East India Company to look for a safe harbour where the
tea- and opium-bearing ships that sailed between Madras
and Canton could be repaired and refitted. It needed a
strategic base east of the Bay of Bengal to protect shipping
during the north-east monsoon because French ships sailing
out of ports on India's eastern coast were harassing the
English in sea battles that mirrored Anglo-French conflict in
Europe and America. During the middle decades of the
century, cargo-laden ships of the Company had to run the
gauntlet between India and the Malay Peninsula, and during
the war for independence in America, where the French
allied themselves with the thirteen colonies against the
British, this harassment continued. To make matters worse,
in 1782–3, and later during the Napoleonic wars, when
Holland was occupied by the French, English ships were
unable to seek refuge in Dutch ports.

Even more important, the Company needed a commercial base for the spice trade and other goods, such as gold,
tin, and birds' nests, which the Chinese wanted in exchange
for tea, silks, and porcelain, as there was no market in China
for British woollens and other goods. A new entrepôt
would stimulate the China tea trade and put an end to the
drain on English silver. Since the British government
imposed a tax on tea, it depended more and more on tea
imports for revenue.

As early as 1771, a suitable harbour had been located by
the young English captain of a ship owned by Madras
merchants trading in the Malay Archipelago. Francis Light,

a 'country trader' operating out of ports in South-East Asia, suggested the island known in Malay as Pulau Pinang to Warren Hastings, then Governor-General of India, so that all English ships, not just those of the Company, could avoid the excessive tolls for repairs and stores charged at Dutch ports.

Light's suggestion to establish a foothold off the Malay coast went unheeded until 1786 when, shocked by the steady damage inflicted by the French, Company officials began to take him seriously. Sir John Macpherson, acting for the Governor-General, finally approved a provisional treaty between Light and the Sultan of Kedah for the transfer of Pulau Pinang to the British crown and the East India Company.

Light's facility with the Malay and Siamese languages, combined with his knowledge of the people and their culture, helped him win their trust. After almost two decades of experience in the region, he also understood regional politics.

During much of the eighteenth century, the Siamese loosely controlled the northern Malay states of Kedah, Kelantan, and Trengganu, but after the Siamese–Burmese wars of the 1770s, they began to tighten their hold on their southern neighbours. When Light approached Abdullah, the Sultan of Kedah, he found a man who saw potential advantages in the new English presence. If the English would pledge to defend Kedah against threats from neighbouring Siamese and Burmese armies, Sultan Abdullah would lease Pulau Pinang to the East India Company for the annual sum of $30,000, the value of the trade in opium, tin, and rattan he expected to be diverted away from Kedah to Penang.

Before a final unambiguous agreement had been signed, Light sailed in three vessels to the island with a small civilian and naval staff. They landed at what is now the Esplanade, in George Town, on 17 July 1786. On 11 August, the eve of the Prince of Wales's birthday, soldiers hoisted the Union Jack over the new stockade and Light took formal possession of the island for the Crown and the East India Company (see Plate 2). He christened it Prince of Wales Island in honour of the man who would eventually be crowned King George IV, and named the new settlement on the eastern cape George Town for the prince's father, George III (Plate 6).

Among Light's first official acts as superintendent was the sinking of a well at one end of what is now Light Street. He also ordered land cleared, but in a letter to Calcutta, quoted in Steuart, he wrote that 'in cutting the trees our axes, hatches and handbolts suffer much … the wood is so exceedingly hard that the tools double like a piece of lead'. While they waited for better tools to arrive from Malacca, as legend has it, Light fired gold coins from a cannon into the thick jungle to hurry the clearing work. Whether true or not, the scramble, as Charles Allen calls it, to find the gold in the jungles of Penang is an apt and prophetic metaphor for future British and other trading interests in South-East Asia.

The ambiguous agreement with the Sultan of Kedah, however, would cast a shadow over the infant settlement. The Company agreed to pay $6,000 annually (Light had suggested $10,000) but it never pledged to defend the Sultan against the Siamese. Ever since 1771, when the East India Company first began its discussions about Kedah and Penang, the Company had vetoed all proposals that might lead to an 'offensive' alliance because of recent conflicts among the peninsular Malay states. Later, after the loss of the American colonies in 1783, England passed Pitt's Act which brought the East India Company under government

6. A view of George Town from Penang Hill which appeared in the *Illustrated London News* in 1876, 100 years after the founding of Penang. (Antiques of the Orient)

control, depriving Calcutta of the power to make any treaty that might lead to war.

Ever since the occupation of Penang, the negotiations between Light, the East India Company, and Sultan Abdullah have been debated by historians. Taking place at a time of molasses-slow communications over vast distances between Kedah, Calcutta, and London, they were characterized by misunderstanding caused by vague language and misrepresentations on all sides. In his eagerness to bring both parties to an agreement, Light played his intermediary role with skill, telling each side what it wanted to hear. He told the Company that the Sultan would accept less than $30,000; then he told the Sultan that the East India Company would comply with the Sultan's request for military aid without informing him of the implications of Pitt's Act. Exactly what the Sultan expected in terms of military assistance—offensive or defensive—against Siam was never made clear.

Some historians support Light, saying he promised to defend Kedah in good faith because he believed it would take much less to defend it from Siamese aggression than the East India Company expected, and that he was deceived by his employers. Others condemn him for errors of judgement, saying that the occupation of Penang was both premature and illegal, and that he had taken advantage of the Malays' naïvety in international diplomacy.

Though Light was now on *terra firma* again, he was, in another sense, cast adrift. For the next eight years Francis Light ran the Prince of Wales Island settlement on a shoestring budget (Plate 7). Months would go by without any communication from Calcutta, making him wonder if the Company had changed its mind about the new venture. When letters did arrive, Company directors expressed second thoughts about its location and harboured unrealistic

7. The East India Company headquarters in Penang, redrawn by David
G. Kohl from an early photograph. (Courtesy of Longman Malaysia)

revenue expectations. Of more immediate concern to Light, however, was the threat of military action from Kedah.

By 1790, the Sultan of Kedah felt betrayed by the British. Since their arrival in Penang he had asked regularly, and in vain, for protection from the Siamese. He determined to win the island back because the East India Company had reneged on its promises. Hoping to force the Company's hand, he enlisted the help of Illanun pirates, who had just driven the Dutch from the Riau islands at the southern end of the Straits, and demanded that the Company either leave the island or guarantee the military aid he had requested and pay a higher annual sum of $10,000.

Getting wind of these plans, Light tried to put pressure on the Sultan by offering to pay him $10,000 after these forces were dispersed. When this failed, Light decided on a pre-emptive strike against the Sultan. Three companies of sepoy soldiers in four gunboats embarked from George Town at four in the morning, landed on the opposite shore, and surprised the coastal fort. With few losses, the English dispersed the larger force collected for its defence, burned two forts, and forced the Sultan to accept British terms: the annual sum of $6,000 and no military protection.

In a caricature of the historical record, with its battles and protracted negotiations, Light was rumoured for decades after his death to have acquired the island from the Sultan as part of his wife's dowry. On the domestic front, however, Light's economic and other incentives would have far-reaching consequences in the Straits.

The new settlement had to attract all its needs—labour, settlers, and capital. Light believed that useful immigrants would not come if government ruled with a heavy hand. In a 1794 dispatch to the Governor-General in Council, Bengal, which is cited in N. J. Ryan's *Malaya Through Four Centuries*, Light wrote: 'Very few people residing here, except the Chulias from India, were ever acquainted with European Governments.... To endeavour to subject these people to our strict military law and discipline would soon depopulate the island of all the most wealthy and useful inhabitants. A mild and at the same time an active government is necessary.' Such a government would turn out to be congenial to the large Chinese community which traditionally kept government at arm's length.

Light believed, too, that traders would take their business elsewhere if the island imposed duties on imports and exports. In order to provide the necessary revenue that would not come from duties, Light made opium available to attract merchants who would distribute it together with other goods further east. The right to make and sell arrack (locally distilled alcoholic spirits) was first introduced in 1789, and an opium farm was established in 1791.

As a matter of policy, the Company had decided to tax the produce of the land rather than sell or rent the land itself for the Company's account. Light insisted, further, that land should be easy for immigrants to acquire. Such an open-door policy, he hoped, would persuade people to come and trade despite the risk of reprisals either from the Dutch or the Siamese.

As a result of these decisions, settlers arrived so fast that Light did not have the staff to do proper land surveying. The Company lured a polyglot mix of Chinese and Indians from Kedah and other Malay and Siamese ports like Junk Ceylon (now called Phuket). Muslim Bugis from Sulawesi, Chulias (a class of Muslim merchant) from India, Arabs, African negroes, Armenians, Persians, Siamese, Burmese, and Sumatrans flocked to the island. Long-time Chinese residents of Malacca also migrated in order to escape the Dutch monopoly.

English trading policies and global strategies had created a need for Penang, but the cosmopolitan mix of Asian immigrants, who outnumbered the Europeans, brought it to life, and made it work. During his term as Lieutenant-Governor at the beginning of the nineteenth century, Sir George Leith, for whom Leith Street is named, would write (as quoted in Ratnam): 'There is not, probably, any part of the world where, in so small a space, so many different people are assembled together, or so great a variety of languages spoken.'

Knowing that such a mixed population could generate tensions, Light adopted the administrative strategy he had observed during his earlier visits to Malacca. He organized the different ethnic groups which settled in the island through 'head men' or *kapitans*—trusted men who were fluent in the dialect of their communities.

The first *Kapitan China*, a wealthy and educated man named Koh Lay Huan, had rebelled against the Manchu dynasty and settled in Prince of Wales Island as a merchant, planter, and tax farmer. His son, Koh Kok Chye, who also got on well with European officials, accompanied Thomas Stamford Raffles to Singapore in 1819.

Beyond his administrative duties, Light and his staff had much work to do. Assisted only by a handful of Europeans and convict labour, Light laid out the first streets of George Town within the commercial area bordered by what are now Light, Beach, and Chulia Streets and Pitt Street, renamed as Jalan Kapitan Kling Mosque. Light and Beach Streets met at the stockade which was soon rebuilt and named for Governor-General Cornwallis (Colour Plate 1).

By 1790, Light was able to report to Company officials in Calcutta that 200 houses with palm thatched (*atap*) roofs had been constructed and drainage work had cleared the swampy foothills. A path had been cleared to the top of Penang Hill. Since he had always hoped that the Prince of Wales Island would grow some of the produce that South-East Asia traditionally supplied to China, he must have been pleased to add that over 1 000 hectares put into cultivation had begun to produce an annual crop of 340 000 kilograms of rice as well as various fruits, coconuts, pepper, sugar cane, and gambier, the extract of which is used in tanning leather, dyeing, and printing.

Light's term as the first Superintendent of the Prince of Wales Island came to a premature end. He never recovered from a malaria attack in 1787, and by the middle of 1794 he was very ill. Eight years after the establishment of the settlement, with its future still in doubt, he asked his good friend and business partner, James Scott, to draft a letter to Calcutta explaining why the Prince of Wales Island was a better choice than Junk Ceylon, which had been occupied in 1787 by the English.

Scott, like Light, was a country trader and sailor before he became a successful merchant. He defended Penang over

Junk Ceylon, insisting that the sailors who complained that the water was too shallow at the northern entrance to the harbour were wrong. Penang was an excellent harbour, he said, with plenty of water, food, and provisions (Colour Plate 2).

Light died at fifty-four, before the Calcutta directors of the East India Company, ending years of ambivalence, had begun to share his commitment to the future of the Prince of Wales Island. He is buried in the old cemetery on Northam Road, now called Jalan Sultan Ahmad Shah.

To his 'fatherly' role during Penang's early days—the Victorian phrase is engraved in the pavilion erected to Francis Light's memory in front of St George's Church (Colour Plate 3)—can be added his legacy as role model for future emissaries of the British crown. Like Light, Stamford Raffles developed a rapport with the Malays and learned their language. He also supported the duty-free port policy, often in opposition to official inertia back home. Together, they secured British control over both ends of the Straits of Malacca. Although Singapore eventually replaced Penang as the capital of the Straits Settlements in 1832, the earlier settlement offered valuable experience to the founders of Singapore.

It would be left to Light's successors, however, to find a solution to the potential danger of allowing one side of the harbour, only about a kilometre and a half away from George Town at its closest point, to fall into unfriendly hands. In 1800, Sir George Leith, then Lieutenant-Governor of the Prince of Wales Island, negotiated a final settlement with the Sultan of Kedah for the acquisition of Province Wellesley, giving Penang control over its harbour and eliminating its dependence on foreign sources on the mainland for much of its food supplies.

from trading for their own accounts. Of course, almost everyone who worked for the East India Company stood a good chance of making money, and Raffles also hoped to retire a wealthy man. But with heavy expenses for his family, and high rents, Raffles, who is quoted in Wurtzburg, wrote home to a cousin in 1806 that he was no better off than before he left England: 'I suppose you are calculating that by this time I am rolling in Rubies, a perfect Nabob, reviling religion and sloughing in immorality. In this however you would be mistaken. I am poorer than I was three months before I left England, and as to splendour and luxury, we have nothing of the kind on our little island; some of the Nuisances with very few of the Comforts are alone afforded us ... I cannot say much for our general appearance of Religion; we have a clergyman but no church.'

The settlement that Raffles found in 1805 would not have an Anglican Church until 1817, but Governor Leith and others had made many improvements. Full of enthusiasm after the acquisition of Province Wellesley on the mainland, Leith, followed by the energetic, spendthrift R. T. Farquhar, concentrated on local affairs and new building.

The government of Penang, under a rapid succession of superintendents, had grown from that of an understaffed Company outpost to a more sophisticated and permanent administration. At a public meeting, leading residents, including the merchants James Scott and David Brown (Plate 9), a Scottish planter at Glugor, elected a committee of assessors, the forerunner of an elected municipal council.

The administration of justice came under scrutiny, too. A lawyer, John Dickens, was appointed to set up a new system for keeping law and order because the small police force that had served the island until now had become

9. David Brown, by an unknown English artist. (Penang Museum and Art Gallery)

inadequate. Major Forbes Ross Macdonald, the island's Superintendent in 1796, who is cited in *Penang Past and Present*, did not mince words about the problems that confronted George Town's expanded police force. He described the town's population as 'a mixed, little estimable population huddled together in a manner little superior to their favorite animal, the buffalo; every species of villainy, of depravity, and of disease here finds asylum'. Many problems within each ethnic community could be solved by its head-man, but in cases of conflict between members of different groups, a magistrate was to be guided in his arbiter role by 'laws of universal and natural justice'.

By 1800, the population of this immigrant society numbered over 10,000, only about 300 of whom were Europeans. But they were a vocal and powerful minority of merchants and planters who could appeal to a higher authority if they disagreed with Company policies, which often sacrificed the welfare of the settlement for business interests of the Company. James Scott, Light's business partner who survived him, was so successful that he was able to buy up the best waterfront property in George Town, west of Fort Cornwallis. He irritated Company officials like the pompous Forbes Macdonald, who disliked Scott's casual style of life. Nevertheless, Macdonald had to admit that although he thought Scott had spent too many years deteriorating among the Malays in the tropics and wearing their *sarong*, he was still an honest man.

Despite these frictions within the European community, progress was evident. Governors Leith and Farquhar built a customs house, jail, and hospital, surveyed the downtown area, and had a grid pattern of streets marked out at 20-metre widths. A road going west from Fort Cornwallis, part of which is now called Macalister Road, terminated at the waterfall in the present-day Botanic Gardens (Colour Plate 4).

Ever since 1795, Penang had served as the penal colony for all of India. Convicts earning enough pocket money 'to furnish themselves with bazaar articles' were employed building and maintaining roads, bridges, and houses. Travellers to old Penang often praised the wide, well-maintained, tree-shaded roads, but they also complained that Penang was a dumping ground for the most dangerous criminals.

By this time, land grants on Jalan Kapitan Kling Mosque, formerly known as Pitt Street, for the present site of the Kuan Yin Temple had been made to the Hokkien and Cantonese communities. Under the leadership of Cauder Mohuddeen, a 7-hectare plot was acquired two blocks away for the construction of a new mosque, the Kapitan Kling (Plate 10), for the growing population of Indian Muslims. The Nagore shrine, built in memory of a Muslim saint, Syed Shahul Hamid, on the corner of Chulia and King Streets was erected at about the same time.

Two blocks away from the Kapitan Kling Mosque stands the Acheen Street Mosque, also known as the Malay Mosque. It was founded by Tengku Syed Hussain, the descendant of a royal Arab family who had come from Acheh, on the northern tip of Sumatra, to settle in Penang during Francis Light's lifetime. Acheh was the main base for Arabs and Indians trading along the spice route, and Tengku Hussain used his entrepreneurial skills to become one of the wealthiest merchants and landowners on the island.

A gala party at the Tengku's home was reported in some detail by the *Prince of Wales Island Gazette* on 7 December 1806: 'The whole of Syed's extensive Premises, as well as the streets and avenues around, were illuminated; Peons were stationed and several officers of the Police attended, for the purpose of preventing the access from being obstructed by the concourse of Native Spectators that had collected to view this, to them, novel entertainment.'

10. The Kapitan Kling Mosque was constructed in 1916 on the same site as the original building. (Major David Ng)

The account goes on to say that dinner 'consisted of every luxury and delicacy that extensive hospitality could procure', the wines were 'excellent and abundant', Malay and Indian dancers provided after-dinner entertainment, and the guests danced until two in the morning.

Such private opulence contrasted sharply with the government's chronic insolvency. After the optimistic days of 1805, Penang would become an expensive burden to the East India Company. Nevertheless, with the arrival in 1811 of James Wathen, word about Penang's charms had begun to spread.

Uncertainty about Penang's future must have been a subject of conversation everywhere James Wathen went when he visited the island in 1811. 'I understand', he wrote in his *Journal of a Voyage to Madras and China*, 'that the East India Company may abandon the island but it will still be a place of interest to people who voyage.'

Wathen had retired at sixty from his profession as a master glover and, obtaining permission from the East India Company, he visited Penang to expand his portfolio as an amateur artist. He was probably the first tourist to visit Penang. Upon his arrival, on 18 September, Wathen saw whales off the coast. He also marvelled at the luminosity of the water and the immense size of the trees. He found plenty of cultivated ground around George Town: pepper, coconut, and sugar cane plantations surrounded elegant garden houses and bungalows. All the roads were lined with a variety of fragrant shrubs and trees (Plate 11). Fruits, vegetables, and excellent fish were plentiful. Indeed, he agreed with the ship's surgeon, James Johnson, who had said in 1805 that 'Penang rivals anything that has been fabled of the Elysian Fields.'

Wandering along Beach Street, he stopped in the Perkins auction rooms which did a brisk business in clarets,

11. Elegant bungalows, set behind tree-lined roads, were—and still are—a feature of George Town. (Major David Ng)

madeiras, jewellery, and sheet music. In town, Wathen would have found other Europeans employed as printers, tavernkeepers, hairdressers, coachmakers, coopers, and watchmakers—trades to be taken over gradually by Chinese immigrants as their numbers grew.

On 26 September he accepted an invitation to dine at Suffolk House (Colour Plate 5), the private mansion of W. E. Phillips, Acting Governor of Penang: 'At seven o'clock we arrived at Suffolk House, which is a very splendid mansion built in a mixed style of English and Indian architecture. The dinner was sumptuous and elegant, and the dessert such as can only be found in a tropical climate. The wines were excellent, the rooms were kept cool by watered mats, and the tables were covered with a profusion of the most odoriferous flowers.'

Wathen went on to name some of the guests, a list of Europeans who were, in his opinion, the only people who mattered. Among them were Dr and Mrs Charles Mac-Kinnon (Colour Plate 6); after dinner, Wathen admired Mrs MacKinnon's drawings of local plants, fruits, and flowers.

Wathen's *Journal* even included comments on how to cultivate pepper and areca nuts. Indeed, the early developers of Penang wanted to fulfil Light's dream of making the island a major production centre for the China spice trade. About 5,000 nutmeg trees and 15,000 clove trees were planted in 1800. James Low, a Scottish civil servant-turned-planter, writing in 1835 noted that two years later another 25,000 seedling nutmeg trees were brought in. Most visitors to Penang stopped at the Glugor plantation to see David Brown's nutmeg and clove trees, for his were the healthiest on the island (Colour Plate 7). Growing these trees was considered tricky on the poor soil of Penang, but with careful cultivation Brown got better results than other planters.

Although the island prospered, it never lived up to the East India Company's expectations. The Company was always trying to cut costs because it could never generate enough local tax revenues. Its well-being depended not only on income from revenue farms but also on London commodity prices, which fluctuated wildly in peacetime. To make matters worse, Napoleon embargoed all trade between Britain and the continent beginning in 1807, so that English exports of spices, pepper, and coffee to France and other continental markets were cut off. Spices accumulated in the Company's London warehouses, and Penang growers, unable to cut costs, faced ruin.

Penang also failed as a shipbuilding centre. Despite the new hopes raised when a British naval expedition set out from Penang to Java in 1811, only one ship was ever built at Penang (Colour Plate 8). Timber suitable for shipbuilding had to come from Burma, but the cattle used to transport it there were diseased. The Company could not find skilled shipbuilders and engineers to build dockyards, and it took too long to get building materials from Europe. Finally, London lost interest in the project and naval stores were transferred from Penang to Trincomalee in Ceylon.

4

Patterns of Change

BY 1835, Penang had grown so much that James Low, the Scottish agronomist, could write that there were twenty-one bazaars, twenty-eight mosques, and fifty-nine native schools where about 600 boys studied Arabic and learned the Koran by rote—'a foolish system of instruction', he added gratuitously. He might also have mentioned that the first English language school in South-East Asia, the Penang Free School (Plate 12), had been established in 1816.

Other important construction had taken place by 1835. In 1805, government buildings were erected on property along the north beach of George Town that once belonged to Francis Light, and Suffolk House was built a few years later as the governor's residence (see Colour Plate 5). The Khoo clan house, known as the Khoo Kongsi, had also been built, following the Cheah and Tan clans which had completed their meeting halls earlier. A Supreme Court building at the junction of Light and Pitt (now Jalan Kapitan Kling Mosque) Streets was put up in 1809, but it was rebuilt in 1905 (Colour Plate 9). Colonel Nahuijs reports, too, that in 1824 there was a Chinese poorhouse and a hospital for local people.

The 1835 census recorded 40,207 inhabitants, with the 16,435 Malays, many of whom had fled to the safety of the island from a Siamese attack on Kedah, outnumbering all other groups. At this time there were 8,751 Chinese, 9,208 Indians, a total of less than 3,000 Arabs, Siamese, Burmese, Parsees, Armenians, Achehnese, Bataks, 'native Christians', and only 790 Europeans.

By 1891, however, the balance between the Chinese and

12. Penang Free School, founded in 1816, was the first English language school in South-East Asia. Part of the original building is now occupied by the Penang Museum and Art Gallery. (Penang Museum and Art Gallery)

the Indian populations in the Malay-dominated ethnic mix had vanished. In the last decade of the nineteenth century, the trickle of Chinese immigrants arriving in Penang had swelled to a tidal wave so that the Chinese constituted half the Penang population. And even though other ethnic groups increased in number, they did not grow as fast as the Chinese. The proportion of Indians in Penang declined from 28 per cent in 1818 to 13 per cent in 1906, which is about where it remains today.

The mostly male Chinese migrating to Penang, as well as to Singapore and Malacca, during the nineteenth century left China for a better life. The Manchu rulers had begun to lose control, especially in the southern provinces, making emigration from poverty, famine, and hardship possible. The lure of wealth and comparative safety under the British flag attracted Chinese willing to tolerate even the most crowded living conditions in their new home.

The British considered the Chinese ideal immigrants because of their willingness to endure hardship, their industry (Plate 13), perseverance, and intelligence, and their ability to organize themselves. Passage was easily available through indentured contractual service arrangements. The opening up of the Perak tin mines under Chinese control in the middle decade of the century proved another powerful magnet to the Chinese.

Although they did not become the largest ethnic group in Penang until the end of the nineteenth century, the Chinese were always visible because of their commercial activities. As early as 1794, in an official report to his superiors, Captain Light remarked on their pecuniary value to the new community: they were 'the only people from whom a revenue may be raised without expense and extraordinary effort of government'.

For Western travellers, however, first impressions of the

13. Chinese water carrier using the *kandar*, a Chinese method of transporting goods, adopted in the Straits. Drawing by Pedersen, 1902. (Antiques of the Orient)

Chinese were not always favourable. The young surveyor–artist, John Turnbull Thomson, writing about his landing at George Town, noticed the 'bald pated, fat, round China men squabbling, screeching, and bellowing in uncouth, parrot-like voices'.

The diplomat John Crawfurd took a more practical—and quantitative—view. He had returned to Penang in 1829 after a ten-year absence and, looking back on his earlier days, he remembered that 'the labour of a Chinese native is worth fifty per cent more than that of a Chulia, and one hundred and twenty per cent more than that of a Malay'. James Low agreed that three able-bodied Chinese workers were equal to five Malays and Chulias. They are 'spirited cultivators', he said. 'But they are prejudiced too', he went on, 'and feel no inclination to raise produce which will not yield a speedy return, such as pepper, sugar, gambier … indigo and vegetables, or to adapt European improvements.'

Scattered over the island as planters, squatters, and farmers, the Chinese also supplied most of its fresh vegetables. But the majority of immigrant Chinese lived in row houses in town, and pursued their traditional crafts and businesses. Vaughan, writing in 1879, said simply that 'the Chinese are everything' and went on to list over 100 occupations (Plate 14). Some lived in rude huts built of bamboo and palm leaves while wealthy merchants built elegant houses with gardens.

John Thomson, a naturalist and photographer who arrived in Penang in 1875, said that a European businessman in Penang cannot operate without a Chinese 'comprador' who pays for produce and collects money for the firm. He was responsible for the purity of the silver in which payments were made. Moreover, a European moving to Penang was completely dependent on the Chinese contractor (Plate 15) to supply all his needs: 'He will build you

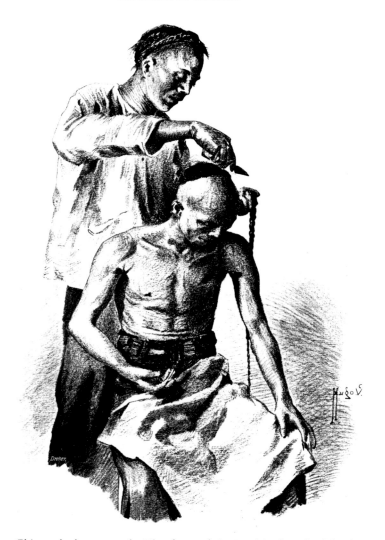

14. Chinese barber at work. The front of the head is shaved while the hair at the back is braided in a pigtail. Drawing by Pedersen, 1902. (Antiques of the Orient)

15. Chinese contractor. (Thomson, 1875)

a house with every speci-fication down to the last nail; his brother will build your furniture; another brother will tailor your clothes; another relative will find you servants and help you get all the European food delicacies on the market.'

As new tin mines opened in Perak, together with smelting operations in Penang and Province Wellesley, the Chinese community of Penang grew wealthy and powerful. Until about 1900, control of the newer tin mines on the peninsula was largely in Chinese hands because their access to cheap labour on mainland China and, for a while, their prospecting techniques helped them compete successfully against the Europeans. If there was a market slump, they could depend for revenue on other sources like the opium and gambling farms which guaranteed a fortune to those who bid successfully for the licence.

By the middle of the nineteenth century, new houses built of brick and tile had replaced many combustible *atap*-roofed houses in George Town, and roads and bridges had been constructed in rural areas. But the physical and economic expansion that lured immigrants to Penang throughout the century did not occur without growing pains—basic services to ensure public health, law and order, and a responsive fire brigade lagged behind.

The convalescing Dutch colonel, Nahuijs, who visited Penang in 1824, found that Europeans always pointed out the health risks of other people's homes, while defending their own as the healthiest in Penang. Yet, the much celebrated climate of Penang Hill (Colour Plate 10), where Europeans sought relief from the relentless heat of George Town, could not save twenty out of thirty-four civil servants appointed between 1805 and 1825. Most of these people died of 'fever' (it was not yet called malaria), dysentery, hepatitis, and drowning, but some died from excessive drinking. Dr T. M. Ward, a 'medical topographer', found that Asians were just as vulnerable as Europeans to 'fevers remittent and intermittent' caused, he believed, by 'exposure to sun and rain, deficient clothing, and imprudent bathing'.

The doctor also blamed the open aqueducts then in use for many health problems. They were frequently made 'the receptacle of every kind of filth', he said. The tides flushed town wastes out to sea through deep drainage ditches, but unusually high tides sometimes brought the sewage back, to the residents' disgust.

The quality of its water supply had been a source of pride to Penang but steps were needed to prevent pollution. To supplement the many wells in use, and to replace the old open aqueduct in use since Farquhar's administration, the government gradually enlarged underground pipes bringing water down from hillside catchment areas, so that by 1887 all principal streets of George Town—and 70,000 people— were provided with safe water.

Other improvements came slowly. New laws passed in the Straits Settlements in 1839 imposed a 10 per cent tax on the assessed value of George Town buildings, but the real administration and direction was left to the distant Governor of Bengal. Later government reforms in 1857 provided new powers to municipal authorities to construct reservoirs, reclaim mangrove swamps, and to clean streets and drains. The government also authorized an annual road tax to finance road maintenance.

Medical advances such as the smallpox vaccine helped reduce mortality rates for adults, but infant mortality remained high, especially for the Asian populations. Ice and cold storage finally became available after the 1860s. By 1908, Penang had a Health Department staffed with ten sanitary inspectors and two medical officers.

Law and order proved a more intractable problem. Iron-ically, a major obstacle to public order were the opium, gaming, and arrack farms—the very sources of revenue the government depended on to provide police protection and other services. Yet the government was caught in a bind because ever since the days of Francis Light it worried that people would leave Penang if opium were not available to attract local merchants. Grown in northern India, distrib-uted throughout Asia in ships of the East India Company, and sold through revenue farms, opium has always raised disturbing moral questions. Since the ruling minority regarded the Chinese and Malays as 'naturally addicted', this conviction made it easier for them to sacrifice principles for profits. In practice, it was Chinese businessmen who, in the annual purchase of opium or gaming farms, made money off the vices, not the virtues, of all segments of the population.

Like any port, George Town filled up with drunken sailors whenever a ship anchored in the harbour. At these times, the police station rang a bell to warn respectable women off the streets. Since alcohol was available in taverns several hours each day, fights often broke out between seamen and the local residents. A law requiring arrack farms to be located at least half a kilometre from the cantonment could not prevent breakdowns in military discipline. Gamblers in arrears organized gang robberies, and the police extorted hush money from those who continued gambling after it was declared illegal.

The Chinese clan system, which settled disputes privately, also frustrated the police because members of the same clan would never testify against or inform on each other. Many clans brought some of their old feuds in China with them, and faction fights broke out again in Penang. James Low wrote that he saw a village after it had been sacked and burned by an opposing clan. The 'Great Penang Riot' of 1867, a gang war between the Hokkien- and Malay-dominated Red Flag Society and the Cantonese-controlled White Flags, left visible bullet marks on houses in Cannon Square, near the Khoo Kongsi.

Fire protection was yet another necessity that the inefficient government could not guarantee. Even after a fire in 1808 destroyed large areas of George Town, the use of combustible materials like *atap* thatching was not prohibited until 1887. In 1848, the *Pinang Gazette* reported that 'four fire-engines were on the ground, but two only would act and the very inadequate supply of water materially interfered with their usefulness'.

For all these reasons, the Europeans began to agitate for change. Residents criticized the Company as an anachronism, arguing that Penang was not part of India and should keep accounts in dollars, not Indian rupees. They were tired of paying for more troops and officers than the island needed. They wanted better services and a more representative government.

At the same time, the East India Company was looking for new ways to economize and simplify its administrative tasks in the Straits. After Bencoolen, in Sumatra, was exchanged with the Dutch for Malacca in 1826, creating separate English and Dutch spheres of influence in the region, the Company united Penang with Malacca and Singapore to form the Straits Settlements and downgraded them from a 'Presidency' to a 'Residency'. Penang remained the administrative centre of the Straits Settlements until 1832 when the seat of government was transferred to Singapore, but it continued as the centre for judicial administration until 1856.

Nevertheless, the Straits Settlements also proved to be an unwieldy creation for the East India Company. The governor and his secretaries shuttled by ship among the three stations: Penang was 433 kilometres north of Malacca, and 633 kilometres north of Singapore. With the expansion of their business interests into new tin mines of the Malayan interior, prosperous merchants and businessmen—both European and Chinese—believed, incorrectly as it turned out, that they could acquire more political control if the Settlements were transferred to the administrative control of the British Colonial Office. Transfer Road, connecting Burma and Northam Roads, commemorates that switch in 1867.

Changes also occurred in commercial agriculture. After a visit to rural parts of the island, John Thomson was convinced he could watch a tropical plant grow with his naked eye. Stems of young bamboo shoots grew 1.5 centimetres in one night, he wrote. Under such apparently favourable conditions, the East India Company had expected to develop Penang into a Garden of Eden, growing spices for the China trade. By 1860, half the island was cleared. Staples like sugar, rice, pepper, coconut, as well as tropical fruits, were grown at sea level while cloves, nutmeg, and coffee grew on the hills (Colour Plate 11).

Such farming dreams, like the earlier optimistic hopes of turning Penang into a naval centre, took no account of obvious soil deficiencies. The island was mountainous and rocky, with only a thin layer of topsoil and alluvial deposits of tin. A long-term investment was required to improve the soil, and the planter got no return until his trees matured. Then, too, planters had to learn the hard way about droughts and plant diseases. Several varieties of nutmeg and mace were grown successfully by the Scotsman David Brown at his large Glugor plantation, but his commercial success was the exception, not the rule.

Buffeted by sudden changes in the commodities markets, planters shifted from one crop to another. When coffee became too expensive to grow, its large-scale cultivation was abandoned. Pepper was discontinued on a commercial scale after it piled up in London warehouses during the Napoleonic Wars. Only Europeans could afford to absorb these losses.

Among the visitors to the tropical plantations of this period was Isabella Bird, a globe-trotting Victorian who wore a pith helmet and a mustard-coloured tweed skirt to match the orange-brown laterite dirt of Malaya. In 1879, she visited sugar, coffee, and pepper plantations on Penang and listed the many products of the island. Among them were guavas, mangoes, lemons, oranges, bananas, plantains, breadfruit, and rice.

Such exploitation of the land took little account of the impact on the environment of deforestation. John Turnbull Thomson may have been the first visitor to notice the clear-cutting of Penang in the 1830s, but he was not the last. Planters recognized early the superior growing conditions on the Hill, and for this and other reasons many trees were cut down. Further down the slopes, indiscriminate cutting by people using charcoal for fuel had destroyed much lush vegetation by 1838. Prohibitions on felling without a licence were not strictly enforced until the 1860s.

James Richardson Logan, a shy but energetic man, took over as editor of the *Pinang Gazette* in 1853. From this platform he raised another lonely voice against the 'denuding' of the eastern hillsides. He emphasized the role of forests in maintaining lower temperatures and preventing streams from drying up. But during the early half of the nineteenth century, many people believed that clearing 'useless' forests was a health and economic imperative.

Planters had to accept changing market conditions, diseases, and droughts, but they also had to cope with shifting trade patterns. Even before the founding of Singapore, in 1819, Penang suffered declines in the value of its trade, but the figures reached a low point in 1831. Siam asserted its influence over the neighbouring Malay states of Kedah and Perak, making investment in the tin business too risky for Penang merchants. Other developments in the region—the British occupation of Java during the Napoleonic Wars, the failure of the Dutch to control disturbances in northern Sumatra, pirates in the Straits, lack of cargo space on ships sailing from Penang to China—all these factors, combined with a temporary restoration of duties on all goods in Penang, contributed to a temporary downturn in Penang's trading fortunes.

After the founding of Singapore, many ships found it more convenient to stop at its deep natural harbour at the pivotal southern entrance to the Straits rather than at Penang, at the edge of the archipelago. Some contemporary observers assumed that Singapore's trade would eclipse Penang's, but others believed, probably in a competitive spirit, that neither Malacca nor Penang lost trade to

Singapore. Rather, Singapore's success may have stimulated Penang to develop new trade routes.

Indeed, Penang's trade revived as Britain extended her influence over Burma and when peace returned to northern Sumatra. As Crawfurd observed in 1829: 'Penang, although it will lose ... the more valuable native commerce that comes from the East, will preserve ... the trade of its immediate neighbourhood, which will embrace the greater portion of the pepper trade, the trade in *Areca* nut, and a very considerable share of that in tin' (Colour Plate 12).

Thanks to the development of steam navigation, commercial and passenger shipping lanes changed during the century, to Penang's advantage. Before the Suez Canal opened in 1869, ships rounding the Cape of Good Hope could use the Sunda Straits, between Java and Sumatra, on the voyage to China. But after the Canal and steam navigation made the trip East both shorter and cheaper, the Straits of Malacca, with stops at Penang and Singapore, became the preferred route to the Far East.

There were good reasons to go to Penang. Besides its coaling services, Penang was also the closest port to the new wealth in tin being extracted from the Malay Peninsula, under new British control. The exploitation of the new tin mines in Perak in the 1860s helped to double trade revenues between 1860 and 1880. Entrepreneurs provided capital investment in the mines in response to the new canning industry in Europe and America. Penang was the closest gateway for importing mining equipment and other provisions for the mines, and for the export of tin ingots. With smelting operations in Province Wellesley and on Penang, and the construction by 1900 of a railroad connecting Penang with Kuala Lumpur, Penang was ready to profit from the lucrative trade not only in tin but also in rubber.

Until the 1890s when the price of coffee collapsed, Henry ('Rubber') Ridley's rubber plant promotions sparked no interest in Malaya. Planters had already discovered, however, that the rubber plant seedlings from Brazil grew better between the mountains and the west coast of Malaya than anywhere else in the world. As the demand for rubber increased with the growth of the automobile industry, prices soared, attracting British capital to form companies with European managers. By 1911, there were 250 000 hectares in rubber and in 1914 rubber earned even more revenue than tin. In less than ten years, the amount of land under rubber cultivation had multiplied four times, the economy of the region was transformed, and Penang's investors and port facilities thrived until the Depression of the 1930s.

5
Destination and Subject

EARLY travellers to Penang were a diverse group. There were the globe-trotters of their day, agronomists, civil servants, engineers, naturalists, tin prospectors, surveyors, and a retired glover. There were also diplomats, naval officers, professional artists, editors, doctors, and convalescents. Amateur artists travelled, too. In varying degrees, they all brought with them their particular European prejudices—what Bilainkin called 'this silly superior feeling'—when they encountered other cultures. Indeed, the written record often tells as much about the viewer as about the view.

Before the camera became a permanent appendage for travellers, even before the picture postcard became the means to share one's travel experiences, Penang was a fascinating pictorial subject. The natural beauty of the island attracted artists whose scenes of the harbour, the hills, Fort Cornwallis, and other points of interest are important visual documents in Penang's history, as well as museum treasures.

Like all tourists, Penang's visitors complained. The hotel was crowded, there was not enough to do, the humidity was oppressive, and the Chinese, according to the Danish artist Pedersen, grabbed every opportunity 'to play tricks on Europeans and stick their fingers in foreign wallets'. They worried, with good reason, about their health. Naturally, they raved about the view from the hills and found the air there refreshingly pure. Many simply enjoyed themselves in their exotic setting, dancing all night with beautiful young women.

There were excellent observers among them, one of

whom was Ambrose Rathborne, a tin prospector who spent fifteen years cutting his way through the jungles of Malaya. Though he claimed to be more comfortable with a *parang* (chopper) in his hand than a pen, his short account of a visit to Penang in 1898 captured vividly the local ethnic drama. He noted the contrast between the Chinese merchants who travelled in equipages drawn by a pair of horses driven by Javanese coachmen and who showed little concern for the 'Chinese coolies toiling in the shafts of jinrickshas'.

He watched the Tamil coolie fawn at the Chetty[1] moneylender—'the bloodsucker of the poor'—entreating him in wheedling tones not to sell his cart and bullocks with which he earned his livelihood. 'But he might as well talk to the granite blocks of which the sea-wall is composed,' Rathborne wrote.

Rathborne was there, too, when the Chinese men watching the English cricket game were almost hit by a ball whizzing past their heads and saw them turn to each other in laughter, congratulating themselves on their narrow escape. 'It never occurs to them to pick up the ball and return it to the players,' he added.

Such details of social interaction—and what happened when East met West on the sports field—were rare. A few artists like the Dane, Hugo Pedersen, and the amateur Edward Cree, among others, drew inspiration from the human aspect of Penang. But most, in the Romantic tradition of the period, concentrated on landscapes that reduced people to dwarf figures, or, like marine artist William J. Huggins, they painted scenes of the harbour and its colourful clipper ships.

---

[1]Also, Chettiar. Member of any of the trading castes of south India who are Hindus.

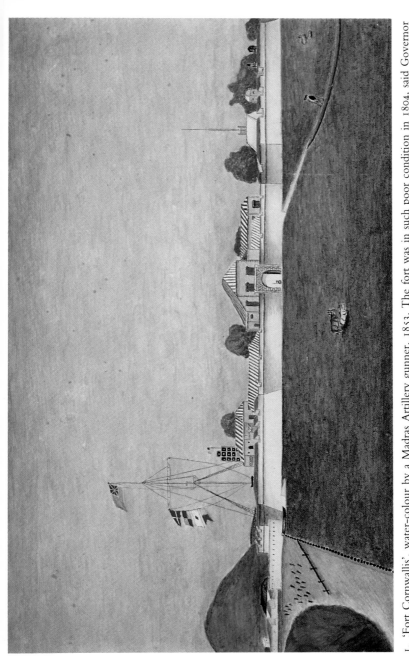

1. 'Fort Cornwallis', water-colour by a Madras Artillery gunner, 1853. The fort was in such poor condition in 1804, said Governor Farquhar, that 'it would not have annoyed one frigate'. (Antiques of the Orient)

2. 'Penang from the Harbour, 1856', water-colour by Captain Charles Henry Cazalet. Flags fly above Fort Cornwallis. (Antiques of the Orient)

3. 'English Church at Pinang, 1848', with the Light memorial, water-colour by John Turnbull Thomson. (Hall-Jones, 1983)

4. 'Cascade à Pulo-Penang', by Admiral Theodore-Auguste Fisquet *c.1836*.
(Antiques of the Orient)

5. 'View of Suffolk House, Prince of Wales's Island', aquatint by William Daniell, 1818. It was probably named after the English county where Francis Light was born. (Penang Museum and Art Gallery)

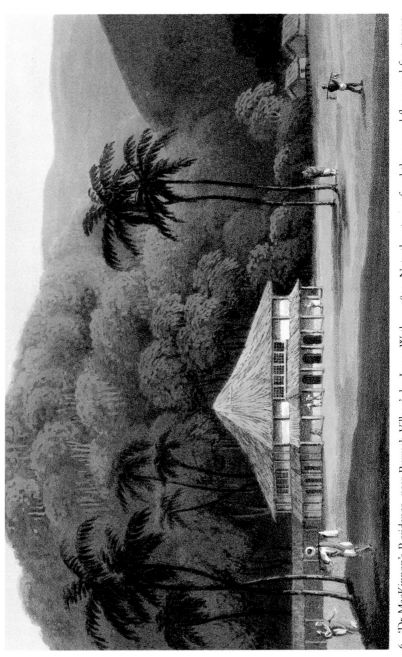

6. 'Dr MacKinnon's Residence, near Burmah Village', by James Wathen, 1811. Note the *atap* roof and the ground floor used for storage. (Antiques of the Orient)

7. 'View of Glugor House and Spice Plantations, Prince of Wales's Island', aquatint by William Daniell, 1818. (Penang Museum and Art Gallery)

8. 'View, looking over George Town, to the Queeda Coast', by James Wathen, 1814. (Antiques of the Orient)

9. Supreme Court House, Penang. (Major David Ng)

10. A European couple relax in the coolness of Penang Hill. (Major David Ng)

11. 'A Sketch on the Pinang Hill', by W. Spreat. (Kinloch, 1853)

12. 'East India Company's Ship *Lord Lowther* Leaving the Harbour of Prince of Wales Island', aquatint by William J. Huggins, 1828. (Antiques of the Orient)

13. 'The Great Tree', aquatint by William Daniell, 1818. This was a favourite spot for picnics and drinking parties during the early nineteenth century. (Raymond Brammah)

14. 'Burmah Temple at Prince of Wales's Island, 1805', by Edward H. Locker. Note the pole, which was one of four that supported a canopy of coloured paper. (Antiques of the Orient)

15. 'Fitting the Young Ladies for Society', water-colour by Edward H. Cree, 1845, whose roving eyes took note of their figures which 'slight clothing and the absence of stays plainly displayed'. (Brigadier G. H. Cree)

16. A luggage sticker c.1920 from the E & O Hotel. (Raffles Hotel Heritage Collection)

Not all visitors to Penang in the first half of the nine-teenth century found its charms so apparent at first as its early publicists, Norman Macalister and Sir George Leith. John Turnbull Thomson arrived as a seventeen-year-old in the late 1830s, and spent a few years there working for his relative David Wardlaw Brown of Glugor estate before he went on to become government surveyor in Singapore. Expecting a tropical nirvana, an 'El Dorado', his memoir written thirty years later described his initial disappointment.

The highlands, he said, loomed 'heavy' and 'shapeless', he recalled, and the once primeval forests had given way to 'mangy patches of scrub and bare stones'. The shore was muddy, fringed with scrubby mangroves, and the eastward view to the mainland consisted of 'a few round ugly hills rising out of a low, swampy, dismal shoreline'. To young Thomson, George Town did not look much better: '... a long line of red tiles with a solitary cocoanut tree sticking up here and there.'

More typical of the first reactions of travellers to Penang around the turn of the century were those of J. Johnston Abraham, the London surgeon who served as a steamship's doctor on a 1907 voyage from Liverpool to Japan. After twenty-one days at sea, he got his first glimpse of the island at dawn: 'The first impression was of a wonderful green; the land seemed smothered in vegetation. It rose precipitous from the water's edge, crag upon crag of naked rock jutting out gray among the green, with here and there the white outlines of verandahed bungalows, perched perilously on the heights, which, half hidden in the verdure, rose higher and higher, and culminated finally in one great peak 2,700 feet above the sea.'

One of the most exciting parts of a passenger's experience occurred once the ship dropped anchor, when the thick

Turkish bath stillness of the air in the harbour became noticeable. Dr Abraham feared pirates were boarding the ship. People—Parsees (Persian refugees who had settled near Bombay), Malays, Klings, Chinamen, and Eurasians—raced each other to be first at the lowered gangway to board the ship and offer their services: change money or sell cigars, fruit, and picture postcards. Sampans (shoe-shaped boats for shallow waters) clustered around the Peninsular and Orient (P & O) steamer 'letting off the sound of bursting firecrackers to frighten away devils that might have slipped unobserved from the steamship onto them'.

Tailors came on board to take measurements for white suits. 'There is something fascinatingly neat and trim in the spotless whiteness and semi-military cut of the dress of the Englishman in the Far East,' observed Dr Abraham. 'Everyone looks well in it.'

Looking around the harbour the new arrival could see 'crazy-looking fishing praus, with bat-wing palm leaf sails, brown and yellow, patched to the limit of patchiness, manned by half-naked, copper-coloured Malays' or dozens of sampans vying for space around the piers (Plate 16).

From the boat the tourist often went directly to Penang Hill. If Thomson sounded grumpy at first, he recovered his enthusiasm on his way to the summit which, at 822 metres above sea level, had cooler temperatures than the plains. He rode a Delhi or Sumatran pony up the path; ladies could ascend in chairs slung on bamboo poles carried by six Tamil coolies. In 1902, Edwin Brown found it an eerie feeling to turn a sharp corner in his sedan chair, 'suspended in mid-air over a sheer drop of up to one hundred feet or more'.

People could also hike to the top for an hour and a half on the trail which started just outside the Botanic Gardens. Since 1923 the trip has been shortened to a half hour by the Penang Hill Railway (Plate 17), but its construction meant

16. Victoria Pier, off Downing Street, George Town. In the 1920s, Sir Frank Swettenham wrote that Penang's harbour had 'scores of every eastern boat that swims, navigated by black and brown and yellow men, in every kind of dress and undress known from Japan to Jeddah'. (National Museum of Singapore)

17. The Penang Hill Railway was constructed in 1923. (National Museum of Singapore)

the demolition of Strawberry Hill, an elegant house that once belonged to the Brown family of Glugor. The same site had been used by Francis Light to grow strawberries and it has now been replaced by a tea kiosk.

At the top of the Hill, Thomson wrote, the air was buoyant, cool, and exciting to the appetite. Distance, he said, 'lends enchantment' to the panoramic views across the harbour to the cloud-capped peaks of Kedah. Colonel Nahuijs, writing in 1824 from his sick-bed at the hilltop home of Norman Macalister, also admired the 'incomparable scene', the tastefully laid out country houses of the Europeans, and the gardens of roses and strawberries. Indeed, Penang Hill had already gained its reputation as a health resort 'far-famed over the East, to which many broken down constitutions resort'.

As a sanatorium, Penang Hill had to lose many of its trees. Trees, it was then thought, contributed to miasma, a disease-causing poison that came from swamps and humid atmosphere. The government also built a convalescent bungalow, with a medical attendant and dispensary, for the use of British army officers and their families on the Hill.

Europeans knew that people living in warm, humid climates had higher mortality rates than those in temperate zones. The heat, they believed, caused changes in the body that weakened it, making it more vulnerable to disease. Before the means to control malaria was developed in 1898, Europeans believed it was impossible to live permanently in the tropics. Since they could not return to a temperate climate every year, they had to make an annual visit for several weeks to hill stations like Penang to regain their strength.

Medical 'experts' had their nostrums: wear absorbent flannel underwear to avoid fever-causing chills and hats to prevent sunstroke. Men should not bathe immediately after strenuous exercise. Refuting rumours about the health risks of Penang, Dr Ward wrote two articles in the *Singapore Chronicle and Commercial Register* in 1833. The people who got sick there, he asserted, were careless with their health by 'going boating and snipe shooting'. For good health, people should 'live on nourishing but not heating diet. Take regular exercise; light a fire; use mosquito curtains; take sometimes a dose of sulphate of quinine, powdered ginger or cayenne pepper at bedtime; smoke a cigar or hookah and preserve confidence and equanimity.'

Sounding more like a poet than a man of science, Dr Ward insisted that Penang Hill was a 'haven of health to the worn-out invalid'. Its atmosphere and the views 'elevate the spirits and render the step free and buoyant'. After assessing the advantages and disadvantages of each summit on the island, he pronounced Mt Olivia, for instance, a 'pleasant little hill' but not a resort for invalids, presumably because a 188-metre altitude was neither high enough nor cool enough.

Penang Hill, also known as 'the Great Hill', and 'Bukit Bendera' (Flag Hill), is the top of the Penang Hill Railway. Early in the nineteenth century the Governor built his stately retreat 'Bel Retiro' on one of the hill's several summits. At 750 metres above sea level and with panoramic views of sea and hills, it was, and still is, an impressive setting for tea parties and official functions.

When Charles W. Kinloch and his wife visited Penang Hill in 1852, they rented a partially furnished bungalow where he slept happily under three blankets. He doubted then that people would be willing to pay the high rates necessary to provision a hotel on the hill. Tourists planning a long stay there, he wrote, should bring plenty of books; except for the 2-kilometre walk from the Great Hill to Western Hill, he found little to do. Unless the visitor 'possess some resource of amusement within himself, he will probably tire of the Penang Hill in less than a week' as there is 'neither society nor amusement on the mountain'.

Although Kinloch was hard to please, he had a point: if one did not enjoy snipe hunting, horseback riding, hiking, or combing mudbanks to collect shells in the hot sun, there was little to do in Penang during the early days. There were, however, some natural attractions to see: the Great Tree, notable for its circumference which was about 10 metres both at its base and 15 metres up (Colour Plate 13); and the Waterfall with its swimming hole, in what is now the Botanic Gardens (see Colour Plate 4). Artists also liked to paint the Burmah Temple (Colour Plate 14) and Mr Amee's flour mill and bakery at the bottom of Penang Hill. People arrived at the mill on horseback and stayed for a tour of the bakery and a hearty breakfast.

A few fortunate visitors, like Edward Cree and John Turnbull Thomson, had introductions to local society where entertainments, public and private, were frequent, brilliant, and lavish. Formal dinners, followed by musical performances by the ladies, began at 4.30 in the afternoon. There were 'few Europeans', Thomson wrote, but they were 'hospitable, social, kind, and agreeable'. Suffolk House, which Thomson described as 'a palatial mansion, with tall, white pillars', 'broad, airy verandahs', and 'liveried servants clothed in white robes, gold-laced turbans, and bright sashes' was the probable setting for a seven-course dinner preceded by sherry and bitters for the gentlemen to whet their 'torpid' appetites. The dining-room ceiling had to be high enough so that the swaying *punkah* fan, suspended over the table and pulled manually, would not disturb the powdered wigs of the guests.

As a naval officer, Edward Cree was invited in 1845 to local dances where he enjoyed dancing all night with young women from a local boarding school who 'never seem to feel the heat although some of us were melting' (Colour Plate 15). At the end of the evening his boots were so saturated with perspiration that he could not remove them without cutting them off in strips.

In 1852, according to Kinloch, 'there was no hotel where a gentleman could venture to shew himself, much less a lady'. But by the turn of the century, this problem had been corrected. A house built on a spur of the hill by a dour Scotsman, Captain Kerr, during the period when the East India Company ran the island, was converted in 1895 to what became known as the Crag Hotel (Plate 18). Ten years later, the Sarkies brothers became its proprietors and ran it in the same opulent manner as their Eastern & Oriental Hotel in George Town. For fifty years the Crag Hotel was renowned in the Straits as a honeymoon resort.

But it was the E & O Hotel which became synonymous with Penang, beginning in 1885 when the Eastern merged with the Oriental Hotel (Colour Plate 16 and Plate 19). It occupied what was probably the longest seafront of any hotel in the world (256 metres) but it was not just its watery setting that made it famous. Its managers, the Sarkies brothers from Armenia, became celebrated hoteliers in the Far East. From the E & O and the Crag in Penang, they went on to establish Raffles Hotel in Singapore and the Strand in Rangoon.

After 1903, when the new ballroom was built, the E & O Hotel became the centre of local social life and Penang offered many new diversions to visitors. A 1924 travel guide to Penang, 'the Pearl of the Malay Archipelago', mentioned the beaches, the Botanic Gardens, churches, the swimming, cricket and golf clubs, and the race course. Man-made wonders were added to the natural ones: the Snake Temple, and the Buddhist Temple Kek Lok Si at Ayer Itam became

18. The Crag Hotel, Penang Hill, was the envy of Singapore where there was no comparable resort. (National Museum of Singapore)

19. A 1909 advertisement for the E & O Hotel, the frequent setting for marriages between colonial civil servants and their English brides. (Antiques of the Orient)

popular excursions. By this time, there were regular con-
certs, a well-established library, and rental cars to tour the
island. In 1908, 5,000 rickshaws registered in Penang were
providing cheap, reliable transportation to all races; a
9-kilometre ride in a first-class rickshaw in 1924 cost 65 cents.

By the 1920s, European residents were more comfortable
in the tropics. They had discarded clothes suitable for a
temperate climate and dressed sensibly in white cotton.
The regular arrival of mail and newspapers kept them in
closer contact with the rest of the world; P & O steamers
made monthly stops at Penang on the way to Singapore,
Hong Kong, Shanghai, and Australia.

Yet despite appearances—servants, large comfortable
houses, and handsome salaries—expatriate life was not easy.
The men found the workload heavy in an enervating
climate. Parents were forced to send their children away to
school in England for long periods. The few women who
came East lived a sedentary life; though some found useful
social work or teaching, many complained of boredom.

Courtship and marriage in the East were complicated.
For a long time, an Englishman risked his job and his place
in European society if he married a local woman. And yet
bachelors found few European women in Penang. 'In the
tropics the simplest looking woman keeps every man on his
mettle, for the plainest woman is a goddess,' observed
George Bilainkin, who was editor of the *Straits Echo* in the
1920s. Married men led a lonely life when their wives
returned to England for a respite from the heat.

One Englishman posted for years to Penang admitted his
homesickness to Dr Abraham: 'At times I long, in a way
you fellows can never understand, for a dish of English
strawberries and cream. I'd give a month's pay for that.'

6

Communities and Cultures

THE melting-pot or mixing bowl images do not provide an adequate picture of Penang. The kaleidoscope, with its shifting intricate patterns of colourful pieces, overlapping sometimes to make new shapes, some larger in one frame and smaller in others, offers a better metaphor for Penang's multiethnic population and its changes over time. Despite the growing pains that accompany modern development, Penang communities have preserved to a remarkable degree their traditional religious practices, language or dialect, clothing, folkways, dietary habits, and economic function.

Malays

'There are two kinds of Malays,' wrote Francis Light in a 1794 dispatch, quoted in Cullin and Zehnder. Referring to the peoples from Sumatra, Java, as well as the Malay Peninsula, Light said that one kind is employed in cutting down wood, at which they are expert, and in cultivating paddy. These husbandmen, he wrote, 'who are quiet and inoffensive, are easily ruled. They are capable of no great exertions, but content themselves with planting paddy, sugar cane and a few fruit trees.... The other order is employed in navigating *prows*. They are in general ... a bad description of people, addicted to smoking opium, gaming, and other vices; to rob and assassinate is only shameful when they fail of success.'

Writing out of his frustration with piracy, Light assessed Malay carpentry skills accurately but failed, so far as the record is concerned, to notice their artistry. The Malays already living on the island when the British arrived in 1786 made their houses of wood. A collection of these houses formed a village, or *kampung*. They were skilled wood-workers—as adept at building houses as making fishing boats. They used *atap*, a material made of palm fronds, to cover the steep roofs which kept off sun and rain, and elevated the roof and the main platform underneath it on posts above the ground, so that open space for storage was created under the house. In a hot climate, Malay houses breathe through attractively carved wooden panels and the slats of the floor.

Kampung could be found where the soil was dry, in shady groves of coconut trees, sugar cane, tamarind, banana, and other fruit trees, but the Malays also needed wet land for rice cultivation. *Kampung* were a popular subject on 1930s postcards for their picturesque swaying-palm-tree charm (Plate 20), but until after the Second World War they were often inaccessible by road and lacked running water, electricity, and sanitation.

James Low, who spoke Thai and Malay, arrived in Penang in 1818 with all the biases of his contemporaries intact. In his description of the Malays he mentioned that they were Muslims, but not 'intolerant, bigoted, or fanatical'. Indeed, Islam was already established in parts of Malaya by the time Marco Polo arrived in the thirteenth century. It was introduced peacefully by Indian traders, missionaries, and conversions associated with royal marriages. During the nineteenth century, Penang became a port of embarkation for *haj* pilgrims bound for Mecca.

Other nineteenth-century visitors like Crawfurd, Rathborne, John Thomson, and Dr Abraham remarked also on the Malay's attachment to agriculture, fishing, and to the water buffalo, which came to symbolize the traditional Malay way of life. Thomson wrote: 'There is a large Malay

20. Palm trees shaded a typical Malay village in Penang. (Major David Ng)

population on the island.... It is, however, a ... difficult task to point out how they are all occupied as they do not practise any trades or professions, and there are no merchants among them. Some are employed on plantations catching beetles, pruning the trees, and tilling the soil; but, on the whole, the Malays do as little work as possible....'

A thriving industry of salted and dried fish, as well as fresh fish, developed in Penang: Malays caught the fish which the Chinese processed and sold. Fishing stakes were visible only at low tide, reported Sir Frank Swettenham: '... the upper half stand above the water, many fathoms from the shore, on the edge of every sandbank.' Along the beach, he added, lie 'black nets and brown nets, of immense length, stretched on a framework of poles—quaint objects and infinitely picturesque'.

Because of his interest in agriculture, James Low must have become a familiar *kampung* visitor, if not always a welcome one; his criticisms ('slovenly', 'unproductive') of Malay agricultural practices seem harsh. In his 1835 book of advice for future planters, he noted the monotony in the Malay diet of fish and rice—a contrast to what he termed the 'extravagance' of their clothing.

Despite the Malay's reputation for passivity, the Malay language spread in Penang and throughout the peninsula. 'The Malay has wakened', wrote Dr Abraham in 1907, 'to find his land taken from him and his country invaded by every nation on earth, and he has shrugged his shoulders and gone to sleep again. But somehow he has imposed his language on the conquerors.' Today, Malay, as well as English, is the lingua franca of Penang, so that one hears it, for example, in conversations between Indians and Chinese.

It could be argued that the Malay language was acquired by necessity, but other aspects of Malay culture— architecture, food, dress, and the *sirih* ritual (betel-nut quid ritual)—were adopted voluntarily by other ethnic groups out of genuine admiration for the Malay's aesthetic sense in all the arts.

The British also admired the pageantry, derived from Indian traditions, that is still associated with the Malay sultanate, and they shared the Malay love of hunting and fishing. They also appreciated the Malays' gentle manner, their courtesy, reserve, and their respect for constituted authority. They were considered good policemen: four out of five law enforcement officers in the pre-war period were Malay. Barefooted, wearing khaki uniforms and black fez hats, they were also good drivers, reported Bilainkin.

The British respected the Malays' way of life—so much so that colonial policy tended to shelter them, encouraging them to remain in their pastoral setting as farmers and fishermen rather than develop ways of competing in an increasingly industrialized world. They still live in the rural areas of Penang, especially on the western and southern villages on the island and commute to work at the modern electronics factories.

Malay cultural traditions vary tremendously within South-East Asia. For instance, certain regions specialize in one decorative craft more than another. The Malay opera (*Bangsawan*) evolved from Hindi plays performed in Penang in the 1870s by visiting Indian troupes, but today it struggles in competition with television. However, an important South-East Asian tradition, the *sirih* offering, has survived as an important aspect of the marriage ceremony. It reflects Malay life as a whole and the value placed by the community on respect for others, refined behaviour, and softness of speech. Batik, the wax-resist method of dyeing cloth in decorative designs, has been an intrinsic element in Indonesian and Malay culture for centuries, and it is now enjoying a revival in Penang.

Chinese

Chapter 4 showed how the Chinese community in Penang grew in numbers and importance during the middle of the nineteenth century. Most Chinese settlers in Malaya came from the coastal areas of south-east China. Settlers from the Teochew province became rice millers and dealers in dried fish and fruits. Possibly because they always wore crisp white clothes, the Hainanese who came to Penang were sought after as servants in European houses and as hotel cooks.

The earliest Chinese settlers at Penang—fishermen and cooks under the East India Company's government—spoke the soft Hokkien dialect. By the middle of the century, they were joined by the Hakka speakers, referred to in Allen as a 'stubborn race of hill farmers'. They immediately antagonized the more settled, less aggressive Hokkiens by opening up new farmland and shops in the middle of the Hokkien community of George Town.

New arrivals from China as well as Peninsular Malaya looked to the transplanted Chinese clan associations for help, protection, and work. In the Straits, clan associations took on this benevolent role for their members, who had a common background. They helped clan members educate their children and pay for funerals. They also promoted harmony among members by settling disputes outside the British legal system, promoting such solidarity within the clan that no member would inform on or testify against another. But problems arose when old feuds from China were brought along to Penang, requiring strong government intervention.

The Chinese also erected clan houses called *kongsi* where clan members could hold meetings and worship their common ancestors. The Khoo Kongsi, for example, is extravagantly Chinese. Built in 1835 in Cannon Square, it is a notable example of traditional clan house architecture in the Straits. Gilded wood carvings and wall frescoes cover the interior walls while multicoloured mythological beasts frolic outside along the roof ridges. Constructed on piers so that the main rooms of the *kongsi* are accessible only by climbing two sets of stairs, it is an example of how the Chinese builders adapted Malay techniques for ventilation and protection from dampness and flooding.

Old Chinese mansions (Plate 21) and shophouses in Penang show a combination of Chinese–Malay and Anglo-Indian architectural influences—an often colourful merging of East and West. In southern Chinese architecture, the gable walls with upturned roof lines and finials were the most important part of a building, whereas the tradition developed by the British in eighteenth-century India emphasized a geometric building mass by using the classical orders, with pediments and porticoes, and decorative corner treatments.

Other Chinese mansions on the island, usually located on tree-shaded avenues on the outskirts of George Town or on Penang Hill, were designed to convey cultural exclusiveness within their own community. They have large gardens with ponds and fruit-bearing trees, marble columns and floors, massive carved wooden doors, and hand-carved ebony furniture inlaid with mother of pearl. Such wealthy merchants' homes, wrote Dr Abraham in 1907, outshone those of what he called the 'dominant race'.

Shophouses in George Town offer a series of narrow façades to the street but stretch back two or three airwells to provide both living as well as commercial space. Penang house interiors have high ceilings, large windows, wide doors, and ornate decorations. The exterior of these colourful buildings reveals Straits Chinese taste: classical Greek or

Roman orders, colonnades and arcades, French windows, cloud-shaped vents, and half-doors (*pintu pagar*) which permit ventilation and privacy at the same time (see Plate 21). Such attention to detail adds visual interest to the urban landscape of downtown George Town.

This eclecticism in domestic architecture is only one example of the Chinese adaptability to their new cultural environment in the Straits. Some, of course, remained traditional and mainstream, speaking their native dialect, wearing a pigtail and Chinese clothing, and sending remittances home to the mainland in anticipation of their eventual repatriation. Others, however, unpacked their bags with the determination to stay in the Straits to make a new life—and a fortune.

Among the Chinese who came to settle permanently in the Straits there developed a unique blend of Malay and Chinese cultures. These people are known variously in the Straits as Peranakans (meaning 'locally born' in Malay), Straits Chinese, or Babas (men) and Nonyas (women). In Penang, Malacca, and Singapore, the Baba community exerted an influence out of proportion to its numbers.

The Chinese who had settled in Malacca after the Portuguese conquest in 1511 had centuries to assimilate Malay culture and develop a special language called Baba Malay. The more recent arrival of the Chinese in Penang, on the other hand, meant stronger family ties to mainland China, which the influx of Chinese labour to the Perak tin mines throughout the nineteenth century reinforced. As a result, the Babas of Penang spoke a musical Hokkien dialect, not Baba Malay.

Like their more traditional Chinese cousins, Babas and Nonyas worshipped Chinese deities as well as ancestors by honouring them on certain festival days and anniversaries, and by maintaining close ties to an extended family. They

21. Yeo Boon Chit's residence in Anson Road is typical of Chinese mansions in Penang, many of which are still standing. (Major David Ng)

were mostly Buddhists or Taoists, but eventually many converted to Christianity under European missionary influence.
Their funerals, especially those of the rich and famous, were
spectacular (Plate 22). The artist Katherine Sim gives an
account of a Chinese funeral procession in Penang of the
1930s: 'It took nearly a half hour to pass—with its long
array of priests and mourners; men in wide flat-brimmed
hats and gorgeous robes, musicians, and hired mourners in
sack cloth, wailing and throwing out paper strips as they
passed to represent money. There were men, women, and
boys, in every variety of costume of the most vivid colours
imaginable, firing now and then an illegal cracker and
carrying laudatory banners....'

The Babas also celebrated important Chinese holidays like
the Lunar New Year, but did so with the preparation of
special Nonya cakes made with coconut milk, brown sugar,
and rice flour, and flavoured with *pandan* leaf. The Chingay
procession and festival, held every two or three years to
honour Kuan Yin, the goddess of mercy, marked auspicious
occasions in the Hokkien community, but everyone in
Penang joined in the fun of watching the colourful flags and
horse-drawn floats go by. Chinese opera, a combination of
mime, dance, and theatre, with elaborate makeup and
costumes, is still part of Chinese festival celebrations in
Penang.

But similarities with the majority of the Chinese
community stops there. Through intermarriage, either with
Indonesian or with Chetty Indian women over several
centuries, some Baba complexions turned several shades
darker than that of the mainland Chinese. Assimilating
Malay culture, Penang Nonyas wore *sarong*, developed a
decorative beadwork and embroidery tradition, adopted the
sirih custom of chewing betel-nut, and learned to cook with
typically Malay ingredients like chillies and coconut milk in

22. Chinese man and boy walking to a funeral, by Barbara F. Shaw, an artist and book illustrator. (Antiques of the Orient)

a distinctive Nonya cuisine. The nearness to Thailand meant that Penang Nonyas also used mint and basil leaves. Modern Nonyas complain, however, that their grand-mothers' gourmet traditions require too much time and work.

In other important ways, the Babas of Penang differed from the traditional Chinese. Because they were socially and economically established, the Babas looked down on other Chinese. They did not join the anti-social secret societies, which had often evolved from the clan associations, and which the British finally outlawed in the 1890s. In addition to Hokkien, they spoke English, and gave their political allegiance to the British colonial administration—so much so that they were called 'the Queen's Chinese'. One English visitor at the turn of the century was amazed to hear a Straits Chinese speak fervently about 'our troops' fighting in the Boer War.

Through education, the sons of Penang Babas developed a broad outlook on the world. They attended the English language schools established in Penang, and later went to England for further education in order to qualify for the colonial service, a source of prestige and influence. Mutual interests were served as the British nurtured a group of hard-working people willing to distinguish themselves from other Chinese by learning English, and, through them, acquired better control over the non-English-speaking Chinese.

Although they adopted English customs like billiards, bowls, and drinking whisky and soda at European clubs, many Babas wore a pigtail, thick-soled shoes, mandarin-style dress, and conical hats. Wedding portraits sometimes show the men in Western suits but they also wore traditional Manchu dynasty gowns while the brides wore Ming dynasty costumes (Plate 23).

23. The 1947 wedding portrait of Mr and Mrs Law Joo Keun shows costumes and head-dress typical of Penang Babas and Nonyas. (Datuk Khoo Keat Siew)

After the war and the decline of British influence, the Babas lost their special position. Many Baba fortunes were lost as well. But political leadership of Singapore and Penang is still, to a certain extent, drawn from the Baba community, and since the 1970s the Babas have been working actively to preserve their rich cultural heritage for future generations.

Indians

A book this size cannot do justice to the rich complexity of the Indian community in Penang. Broadly, it is divided into Muslims and Hindus, from north India (Bengalis, for example) and south India (Tamils). Among the north Indian Hindus, there are Hindustanis and Sindhis. Muslims from the northern part of the subcontinent include Gujeratis (Bombay) and Pakistanis. There are many other categories along linguistic, ethnic, educational, and caste lines. Their occupations in Penang range from the dhobis who take in laundry to university professors, doctors, and lawyers.

Most Indians who arrived in Penang came from south India and spoke Tamil. They came not only as convicts but also as indentured workers and independent merchants. In the nineteenth century and early decades of the twentieth, almost all Indians in the Malay Archipelago were known as 'Klings' (Plate 24) a word derived from the old name for a strip of the south-east Indian coast called Kalinga. The term 'Kling' has now been replaced by 'Tamil'. The first mosque built in Penang is still known by its old name, the Kapitan Kling.

Until the mid-nineteenth century, Penang served as India's penal colony. The convict's crime was branded on his forehead in two languages. Prisoners contributed their labour to building and maintaining roads, brick-making,

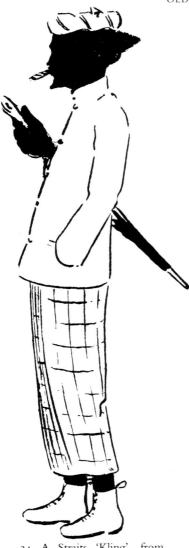

24. A Straits 'Kling', from Stirling, 1923. (Antiques of the Orient)

filling in swamps, and the construction of public buildings and aqueducts. If they stayed on and married local Malay women after serving their sentences, Indians in Penang still had difficulty removing the stigma of a prison record. For a long time, Europeans regarded Indians with suspicion.

In his 1794 dispatch appealing for better law enforcement authority, for example, Francis Light wrote that the East India Company brought between 1,500 and 2,000 Indians to the settlement annually 'none worthy of much confidence'. When James Wathen travelled to Penang on a ship carrying forty convicts from Madras, he let appearances be his guide: some were 'decent looking', he wrote, but others 'Nature had marked for villainy in every feature'.

Daily contact with convicts, combined with distance from home, may have had an adverse effect on the character of other Indians from Madras and Bengal, wrote James Low in 1836. Their conduct had become lax and, although it is not clear how a non-Indian like Low would know much about such things, they had 'lost caste', he said. Except for George Bilainkin, who worked with a broad spectrum of Penang's population at the *Straits Echo*, Europeans rarely mentioned the English-speaking Indian employees they must have encountered in government offices and on the railroads during their travels.

The English, it seems, were hard to please. They complained that the Chinese were inveterate gamblers and opium addicts, but at the same time they had little use for Indians who did not contribute to the public coffers by patronizing these same revenue farms, diligently saving their money instead. 'No class of men can here subsist on less than a Chuliah can,' wrote James Low. Indians sent home savings from their work as boatmen, grooms, shopkeepers, or as drivers of bullock carts.

Much later, during the rapid expansion of the rubber plantations in mainland Malaya, Penang became the main port of entry for indentured rubber estate workers with free passage from India. English managers considered the Indians good workers, 'easily manageable', and 'well suited to regimented estate life'.

Today, the centre of the Indian community in George Town is located in Jalan Kapitan Kling, and King, Queen, Market, and Penang Streets. Church and Bishop Streets are home to wealthy Indian and Chinese merchants. Across from the Kapitan Kling Mosque, Indian Muslim money-changers and goldsmiths are open for business. Chettiar moneylenders work at various downtown locations away from the mosque. For Muslims, the 29-day fasting month of Ramadan, followed by the Hari Raya Puasa festival, is the focal point of the holy calendar.

Finding the Malay culture, religion, and no-pork dietary habits congruent with their own, Indian Muslims have identified with the Malays. Intermarriage between them has produced another group of people called Jawi-Peranakans. Although they all consider themselves Malaysian citizens, many Indians of today's older generation still maintain close ties with their ancestral roots in India.

The Hindus of Penang, who are slightly outnumbered by the Indian Muslims, celebrate a unique festival called Thaipusam on a date set according to the Tamil–Hindu Lunar calendar. The three-day celebration originated in south India where Lord Subramaniam, a god in the Hindu pantheon, is especially popular, but it is no longer observed on this elaborate scale in India. The festival honours Subramaniam, the son of Shiva and the destroyer of evil.

After weeks of fasting and abstinence, participants in Thaipusam carry out vows of penance in hopes of having a favour—the recovery of a sick relative, for example—granted. The majority of devotees carry a container of milk on their heads as they walk the roughly 2-kilometre path between two temples—from Sri Mariamman in Queen Street to the Nattukkotai Chettiar Temple in Waterfall Road (Plate 25). But others in a state of trance carry decorated yokes called *kavadis*, with their cheeks and tongues skewered by spikes and their chests pierced by small hooks, a lime hanging from each barb. Devotees, it is said, feel no pain.

There is also a sizeable population of Sikhs in Penang. Emily Richings, quoted in Donald Moore, came to Penang in 1909 and commented on 'noble-looking Sikhs, in spotless linen, striding past in kingly gait'. The centre of all Sikh religious activity is a temple in Brick Kiln Road.

There are many different Indian foods available in Penang. Among the specialities are *roti canai*, unleavened bread unique to Indian Muslims in the Malay Peninsula, and

25. Brahmin (Hindu) priests at the Nattukkotai Chettiar Temple in Waterfall Road use sacred marks on their faces. (Antiques of the Orient)

murtabak, Indian-style pizza filled with minced mutton, onions, and eggs and fried over a hot metal plate.

Thais and Burmese

Emily Richings also noticed the Siamese during her 1909 trip to Penang. 'Brown Siamese', she wrote, 'in many coloured scarves and turbans gleaming with gold thread, chaffer and bargain at open stalls with blue-robed Chinamen.'

More numerous in the past, the Siamese, called Thais since 1949, have dwindled now so that they, together with Eurasians, Arabs, and Burmese, number less than 1 per cent of Penang's population. But Penang's Thai Buddhist temples, especially Wat Chayamangalaram in Pulau Tikus, is evidence of the Thai community's historical importance on the island. Built in 1845 on a site donated by Queen Victoria, the temple claims to have the third largest reclining Buddha in the world. Legends of the Buddha's life are painted on interior walls by Thai artists.

Thai culinary traditions have influenced Penang's own cooking styles in the use of lemongrass (*serai*) and chillies. *Laksa* (noodles in a spicy fish soup) was originally a Thai dish that has been modified in Penang, using coconut milk (*laksa lemak*) or tamarind (*laksa asam*) for flavouring. The creamy *laksa lemak* and the more sour-tasting *laksa asam* are typical Penang fare.

About a hundred Burmese, mostly fishermen and farmers, settled on Penang after the British arrived. Land for the Burmese Dhammikarama Buddhist Temple was acquired through Governor Leith in 1803. Two large stone elephants mark the entrance located across Lorong Burma from the Thai temple. The Burmese community lived at the end of the Burmah Road but most Burmese today have been assimilated through intermarriage.

Eurasians

Early travellers to South-East Asia were mystified to find what one called this 'new kind of man'. John Thomson mentioned a man claiming Portuguese descent who wore a chimney pot beaver hat. Many Eurasians of Portuguese or Dutch descent came with Francis Light from Junk Ceylon and Kedah. Eventually, Portuguese Christians founded the Cathedral of the Assumption in the heart of George Town. At one time, Eurasians lived in Argus Lane but today the community's centre is Pulau Tikus, on the north-west outskirts of George Town. Most Eurasians speak both English and Malay.

Arabs

For centuries Acheh, in northern Sumatra, was an important Arab centre for the spice trade and religious studies. It served as a link between South-East Asian ports and the Middle East, and as a point of departure for the annual pilgrimage to Mecca. And it was from Acheh that Tengku Syed Hussain, referred to in Chapter 3, came to Penang in 1792.

Francis Light was so eager to have the Tengku and his clan settle in Penang that he granted him exemption from British laws. Light reported that the Arabs are 'strict Mohamedans who trade with all countries; they are good friends and dangerous enemies'. For their part, the Arabs discovered their affinity with the Malay customs, foods, and lifestyles in Penang.

Acheh was the continuing source of much Arab immigration to Penang, which accelerated during the nineteenth century disturbances there. Later Arab immigrants came directly from Mecca in Saudi Arabia, South Yemen, or through Singapore. If they were not Arab sheikhs or merchant princes like the Tengku, they were traders or religious teachers and leaders.

Acheen Street in the heart of George Town belonged to Tengku Hussain and his merchant friends. They owned several buildings which they used for storing, processing, and trading spices. In 1916, an Arab school was set up here, for the Achehnese Arabs brought with them a deep respect for education.

7
Epilogue

LESS than 200 years after the British East India Company arrived to claim it as a mercantile and naval centre, Penang—the island and Province Wellesley, now known as Seberang Prai—became one of independent Malaysia's thirteen states. Independence—(*merdeka* in Malay)—came only twelve years after the Union Jack replaced the Japanese flag over Fort Cornwallis.

It is beyond the scope of this short book to comment on the $3\frac{1}{2}$-year Japanese occupation of Malaya and the 10-year political and military struggle against the Communist insurgency that followed the war. It has been difficult to focus exclusively on the island of Penang, so it may be useful, now, to look at it as a part of the Malaysian federation, and then to see how the colonial past survives in modern Penang.

The choice of an island underlines the British intention to avoid entanglements on the mainland beyond the acquisition of Province Wellesley to protect Penang's harbour. To the eighteenth-century sultans of Kedah, however, even a sparsely populated and densely forested Penang Island was always part of the main, and the 13.5-kilometre bridge opened in 1985, which now links it like an umbilical cord with Butterworth, is the obvious symbol of its close ties with the peninsula.

Unlike Singapore, an island state that controls its own destiny under a Chinese majority, Penang has become part of a larger and quite different nation. As the only state among Malaysia's thirteen with a clear non–Malay majority,

Penang has had to adjust to a new reality. Political power under Malay leadership resides in Kuala Lumpur, and policies formulated at the federal level have an impact on all the states. Today, the government tries to help Malays acquire the economic skills to prosper in the industrialized global marketplace through the New Economic Policy. Inaugurated in 1970, the NEP aims to eliminate poverty and to promote Malay economic interests.

Lacking the natural resources like timber, rubber, and tin that have enriched other states, Penang has capitalized on its skilled population by inviting multinational investment to the island. Modern Penang is the most industrialized Malaysian state, receiving more revenue from industry than from commodities. Penang provides jobs in electronic and rubber-based industries and tin smelting for workers from all over the region, who send remittances home; at the same time, substantial numbers of the Penang workforce migrate to other parts of the country, especially to Kuala Lumpur, in a two-way migration that keeps the island's population stable.

Although almost anything will grow these days on Penang, commercial agriculture is limited. Only durians (a large fruit native to tropical Asia), nutmeg, cloves, vegetables, bananas, cocoa, and coconut trees, and a small amount of rubber are cultivated on very small island holdings. There is also some rice farming, as well as a rice mill, but most of Penang's rice is now imported from Thailand.

The early introduction of English education, and the continued exposure to Western ideas, helped create a middle class in Penang long before it developed elsewhere in the peninsula. Penang schools are more democratic today, less élitist than in the past. Unlike the middle class in Kuala Lumpur, which has strong ties to the federal government,

Penang's is more autonomous and independent. Not surprisingly, Penang is a haven for artists and reformers who, being out of tune with the political mainstream of Malaysia, have been described as the nation's conscience.

Industrialization and tourism have meant continuing changes: Penangites move to high-rise condominiums, Malay fishermen leave their *kampung* to make way for hotels, hilltops are cleared and flattened for housing estates, and paddy-fields are drained for industrial development. In 1990, the annual number of visitors to Penang was twenty times larger than in 1970. But much of old Penang survives if one knows where to look.

In the shadow of the 65-storey Komtar office building which towers over George Town, the owner of a dim pawnshop does calculations on an abacus, a street cook manually fans the charcoal fire under his wok, and a Chinese trishaw driver takes a midday nap in the shade of its hood as the call to prayer sounds from a nearby mosque. On a sidewalk, Burmese sesame seeds dry in the sun on a piece of burlap.

In the more suburban and rural areas, the older generation meets informally on Gurney Drive for an invigorating walk in the early morning sea breeze—and for a gossip. A coastline drive to the lighthouse at Muka Head or to the fishing village at Gertak Sanggul passes pristine beaches edged with palm trees. Time has stood still in some corners of Penang.

The colonial past, too, lingers on in various ways. There are over 100 streets named for English civil servants and headmasters, but these are gradually being renamed to recognize the achievements of Penangites. The Anglo-Indian architecture of prominent buildings attracts movie-makers in search of authentic colonial sets. Tourists perch on the old cannons at 'Kota Cornwallis' and photograph the Clock Tower at 'Pesara Raja Edward'.

In less obvious ways, British influence is still felt in Penang. Francis Light's grid street plan in George Town endures, and George Town's municipal administration set up by the British has been a blueprint for other cities in Malaysia. Because English has been the language of instruction in the missionary schools, Penang graduates have had access to international careers in the professions, business, and politics. But perhaps the most enduring legacy of the colonial period is the kaleidoscopic diversity of its population—which seeks unity, not uniformity, out of shared values.

Modern urbanization and economic development have been a mixed blessing for Penang. The rapid construction of hotels in Batu Ferringhi has seemed to strain the island's resources to manage such changes. One often hears complaints about flash floods, soil erosion, and the draining of raw sewage into the sea. Penangites worry, too, about the unforeseen environmental impact of a land reclamation project on the north-eastern coast that will probably alter the turtle shape of the island.

Yet state government officials recognize the need now to address environmental issues and the quality of life. More sewage treatment plants, for example, are planned throughout the state. The Municipal Council has identified five historic areas of George Town and published building guidelines so that new construction, it is hoped, will not disturb the low-rise human scale of historic George Town. The recent purchase of the Cheong Fatt Tze Mansion for restoration raises hopes that others, such as the now derelict Suffolk House, will get attention as Penang comes to terms with a past that is a unique blend of both East and West—and capitalizes on it.

In this age of mass tourism, Penang Hill is more popular than ever as a vacation retreat. A challenge for the future is to meet those new demands while at the same time respecting the hill's fragile ecology and water catchment areas so that the island's magnificent natural heritage can be protected for future generations.

Select Bibliography

Abraham, J. Johnston, *The Surgeon's Log*, London, Chapman and Hall, 1911.

Allen, Charles (ed.), *Tales from the South China Seas*, London, Andre Deutsch & BBC, 1983.

Andaya, Barbara Watson and Andaya, Leonard, *A History of Malaysia*, London, Macmillan, 1982.

Bassett, D. K., *British Trade and Policy in Indonesia in the late 18th Century*, Hull, University of Hull, 1971.

Bastin, John and Winks, Robin W. (eds.), *Malaysia: Selected Historical Readings*, Kuala Lumpur, Oxford University Press, 1966.

Bilainkin, George, *Hail Penang!*, London, Sampson Low, 1932.

Bird, Isabella L., *The Golden Chersonese and the Way Thither*, London, Murray, 1883; reprinted Kuala Lumpur and Singapore, Oxford University Press, 1967 and 1989.

Bonney, Rollins, *Kedah 1771–1821: The Search for Security and Independence*, Kuala Lumpur, Oxford University Press, 1971.

Brown, Edwin A., *Indiscreet Memories*, London, Kelly & Walsh, 1936.

Butcher, John G., *The British in Malaya 1880–1941*, Kuala Lumpur, Oxford University Press, 1979.

Cameron, John, *Our Tropical Possessions in Malayan India*, London, Smith, Elder & Co., 1865; reprinted Kuala Lumpur, Oxford University Press, 1965.

Clammer, John R., *The Ambiguity of Identity: Ethnicity Maintenance and Change Among the Straits Chinese Communities of Malaysia and Singapore*, Singapore, Institute for Southeast Asian Studies, 1979.

_____, *Straits Chinese Society*, Singapore, Singapore University Press, 1980.

Cowan, C. D. (ed.), 'Early Penang and the Rise of Singapore

(1805–1832)', *Journal of the Malayan Branch of the Royal Asiatic Society*, March 1950.

Crawfurd, John, *Journal of an Embassy from the Governor-General of India to the Courts of Siam and Cochin China*, London, Colburn, 1828; reprinted Kuala Lumpur and Singapore, Oxford University Press, 1967 and 1987.

Cullin, E. G. and Zehnder, W. F., *The Early History of Penang, 1592–1827* (reprinted from the *Straits Echo*), Penang, The Criterion Press, 1905.

Davies, Donald, *Old Penang*, Singapore, Donald Moore, 1956.

Ghulam Sarwar Yousof, *Ceremonial and Decorative Crafts of Penang*, Penang Museum, 1986.

Gwee Thian Hock, *A Nonya Mosaic*, Singapore, Times Books International, 1985.

Hall-Jones, John, *The Thomson Paintings: Mid-Nineteenth Century Paintings of the Straits Settlements and Malaya*, Singapore, Oxford University Press, 1983.

Khoo Kay Kim, *The Western Malay States 1850–1873*, London, Oxford University Press, 1972.

Kohl, David G., *Chinese Architecture in the Straits Settlements and Western Malaya*, Kuala Lumpur, Heinemann Asia, 1984.

Kinloch, Charles W. [Bengal Civilian], *Rambles in Java and the Straits in 1853*; reprinted Singapore, Oxford University Press, 1987.

Lim Chong Keat, *Penang Views 1770–1860*, Singapore, Summer Times Publishing, 1986.

Low, James, *A Dissertation on the Soil and Agriculture of the British Settlement of Penang ...*, Singapore, Singapore Free Press, 1836; reprinted Singapore, Oxford University Press, 1972.

Moore, Donald, *Where Monsoons Meet*, London, G. G. Harrap & Co., Ltd., 1956.

Nahuijs, Colonel, 'Letters to Lt. Gov. of Netherlands Indies, 1824', *Journal of the Malayan Branch of the Royal Asiatic Society*, 19 (2), 1941.

Ng, Major David and Tate, Muzaffar D. J., *Malaya Gaya Hidup 1900–1930*, Petaling Jaya, Penerbit Fajar Bakti Sdn. Bhd., 1989.

Pedersen, Hugo V., *Door Den Oost-Indischen Archipel*, Haarlem, H. D. Tjeenk Willink & Zoon, 1902.

Penang Past and Present 1786–1963: A Historical Account of the City of George Town Since 1786, 1966.

Prince of Wales Island Gazette.

Pulau Pinang.

Purcell, V. W. W. S., *Early Penang*, Penang, Gazette Press, 1928.

Rathborne, Ambrose B., *Camping and Tramping in Malaya*, London, Swan Sonnenschein, 1898; reprinted Singapore, Oxford University Press, 1984.

Ratnam, Margaretha, *Penang*, Petaling Jaya, W. D. Andreae, 1973.

Ryan, N. J., *Malaya Through Four Centuries*, Kuala Lumpur, Oxford University Press, 1959.

_____ , *The Cultural Heritage of Malaya*, Singapore, Longman Malaysia, 1962.

_____ , *A History of Malaysia and Singapore*, London, Oxford University Press, 1976.

Sim, Katherine, *Malayan Landscape*, London, Michael Joseph Ltd., 1946.

Scott, James, 'Historical Sketch of Penang in 1794', John Bastin (ed.), *Journal of the Malaysian Branch of the Royal Asiatic Society*, 32 (1), May 1959.

Steuart, A. Francis, *A Short Sketch of the Lives of Francis and William Light*, London, Sampson Low, 1901.

Stirling, W. G., *Shadows on a Malayan Screen*, Singapore, Kelly and Walsh, 1923.

Swettenham, Sir Frank, *British Malaya*, London, John Lane, 1907; rev. edns., London, Allen & Unwin, 1929 and 1948.

Thomson, John, *The Straits of Malacca, Indo-China and China*, London, Sampson Low, 1875.

Thomson, John Turnbull, *Some Glimpses into Life in the Far East*, London, Richardson & Co., 1865; reprinted Singapore, Oxford University Press, 1984.

Turnbull, C. M., *The Straits Settlements 1826–1867*, London, Athlone Press, 1972.

_____, *A History of Malaysia, Singapore, and Brunei*, London, Allen & Unwin, 1989.

Vaughan, Jonas Daniel, *The Manners and Customs of the Chinese of the Straits Settlements*, Singapore, Mission Press, 1879; reprinted Kuala Lumpur, Oxford University Press, 1971.

Ward, T. M., 'Medical Topography of Pinang and Province Wellesley', *Singapore Chronicle and Commercial Register*, 18, 25 July and 1 August 1833.

Wathen, James, *Journal of a Voyage to Madras and China*, London, 1814.

Wong Lin Ken, 'The Revenue Farms of Prince of Wales Island 1805–1830', Ph.D. dissertation, University of Malaya (Singapore), 1954.

Wright, Arnold and Cartwright, H. A. (eds.), *Twentieth Century Impressions of British Malaya*, London, Lloyd's Greater Publishing Co., Ltd., 1908.

Wurtzburg, C. E., *Raffles of the Eastern Isles*, London, Hodder & Stoughton, 1954; reprinted Singapore, Oxford University Press, 1984.

Yeap Joo Kim, *The Patriarch*, Singapore, Times Books International, 1984.

Index

94

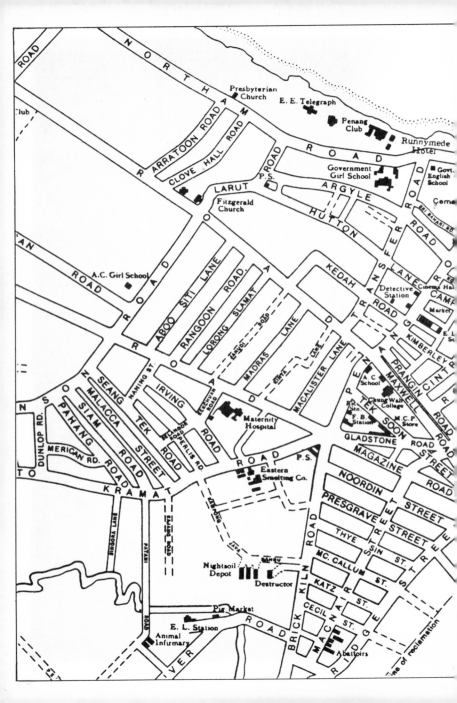